SCHOOLS AND QUALITY

An International Report

ORGANISATION FOR ECONOMIC CO-OPERATION AND DEVELOPMENT

Pursuant to article 1 of the Convention signed in Paris on 14th December 1960, and which came into force on 30th September 1961, the Organisation for Economic Co-operation and Development (OECD) shall promote policies designed:

- to achieve the highest sustainable economic growth and employment and a rising standard of living in Member countries, while maintaining financial stability, and thus to contribute to the development of the world economy;
- to contribute to sound economic expansion in Member as well as non-member countries in the process of economic development; and
- to contribute to the expansion of world trade on a multilateral, non-discriminatory basis in accordance with international obligations.

The original Member countries of the OECD are Austria, Belgium, Canada, Denmark, France, the Federal Republic of Germany, Greece, Iceland, Ireland, Italy, Luxembourg, the Netherlands, Norway, Portugal, Spain, Sweden, Switzerland, Turkey, the United Kingdom and the United States. The following countries acceded subsequently through accession at the dates indicated hereafter: Japan (28th April 1964), Finland (28th January 1969), Australia (7th June 1971) and New Zealand (29th May 1973).

The Socialist Federal Republic of Yugoslavia takes part in some of the work of the OECD (agreement of 28th October 1961).

Publié en français sous le titre:

LES ÉCOLES ET LA QUALITÉ

© OECD, 1989
Application for permission to reproduce or translate all or part of this publication should be made to:
Head of Publications Service, OECD
2, rue André-Pascal, 75775 PARIS CEDEX 16, France.

The need to enhance the quality of education, especially in primary and secondary schools, has become a dominant theme of policy and debate in the educational field across the majority of OECD countries. This need was a major subject for discussion by the OECD Ministers of Education when they last met in Paris in November 1984. They recommended that the Education Committee incorporate analysis and exchange of information on "the quality of basic schooling" as a key element of its subsequent work. This report is the culmination of that work.

From the outset, it became clear that an international enquiry into schools and quality must meet two distinct demands. First, there is the need to engage in the conceptual, even philosophical, exercise of clarifying the nature of quality as applied to the educational field, and of examining the reasons why it has emerged so prominently as a defining goal of contemporary policy-making. Second, there is the need to address developments, issues, and problems as they have emerged across OECD countries in those concrete policy fields most directly pertinent to the pursuit of quality. This report is divided accordingly into two parts corresponding to these distinct demands, in addition to a final chapter of summary and conclusions.

The main authors of this report are John Lowe, now retired from the OECD staff, and David Istance of the Education and Training Division in the Directorate for Social Affairs, Manpower, and Education. They drew substantially on the results of international conferences organised as an integral part of the programme on quality on specific topics reflected in the chapters of Part Two. An important contribution to its preparation was made by Professor Denis Lawton, Director of London University's Institute of Education.

The report is published on the responsibility of the Secretary-General.

Also available

EDUCATION AND THE ECONOMY IN A CHANGING SOCIETY (1989)
(91 88 03 1) ISBN 92-64-13176-0   102 pages
£10.00   US$17.00   FF80.00   DM33.00

PATHWAYS FOR LEARNING. Education and Training from 16 to 19 (1989)
(91 88 02 1) ISBN 92-64-13175-2   124 pages
£10.00   US$19.00   FF85.00   DM37.00

ONE SCHOOL, MANY CULTURES (1989)
(96 89 01 1) ISBN 92-64-13195-7   80 pages
£8.50   US$15.00   FF70.00   DM29.00

NEW TECHNOLOGIES IN THE 1990s: A Socio-Economic Strategy (1989)
(81 88 07 1) ISBN 92-64-13180-9   126 pages
£11.00   US$19.00   FF90.00   DM37.00

MULTICULTURAL EDUCATION (1987)
(96 87 03 1) ISBN 92-64-12989-8   350 pages
£12.00   US$25.00   FF120.00   DM52.00

IMMIGRANTS' CHILDREN AT SCHOOL (1987)
(96 87 02 1) ISBN 92-64-12954-5   322 pages
£12.00   US$22.00   FF120.00   DM44.00

INFORMATION TECHNOLOGIES AND BASIC LEARNING. Reading, Writing, Science and Mathematics (1987)
(96 87 05 1) ISBN 92-64-13025-X   270 pages
£15.00   US$32.00   FF150.00   DM65.00

GIRLS AND WOMEN IN EDUCATION. A Cross-national Study of Sex Inequalities in Upbringing and in Schools and Colleges (1986)
Out of print. Available on microfiches (2)
Prices per microfiche:
£2.50   US$4.50   FF20.00   DM8.00

* * *

OECD: EMPLOYMENT OUTLOOK. September 1988
(Chapter 2, in particular, focuses on new cross-country evidence on youth labour market and schooling activity.)
Out of print. Available on microfiche (3)
Prices per microfiche:
£2.50   US$4.50   FF20.00   DM8.00

To be published

EDUCATION IN OECD COUNTRIES 1986-1987: COMPARATIVE STATISTICS

Prices charged at the OECD Bookshop.
THE OECD CATALOGUE OF PUBLICATIONS and supplements will be sent free of charge on request addressed either to OECD Publications Service,
2, rue André-Pascal, 75775 PARIS CEDEX 16, or to the OECD Distributor in your country.

TABLE OF CONTENTS

INTRODUCTION 9

Part One
QUALITY: THE CONCEPT AND THE CONCERN

Chapter 1. REASONS FOR THE CURRENT INTEREST IN QUALITY 15
  Introduction 15
  Reactions to the Era of Growth 15
  Schools and Teachers in Question 17
  Quality in Education and Economic Imperatives 19
  The Social Context of Schools 22
  Concluding Remarks 24
  Notes and References 25

Chapter 2. THE CONCEPT OF QUALITY 27
  Introduction 27
  Quality — the Word 27
  Quality in Schooling: Dimensions and Approaches 29
  a) Style of enquiry and level of schooling addressed 29
  b) Goals and objectives 30
  c) Quality of what? 31
  d) Quality for whom? 33
  Concluding Remarks 35
  Notes and References 36

Chapter 3. THE CONTROVERSIAL ISSUE OF STANDARDS 37
  Introduction 37
  The Meaning of Standards 37
  Methodological Problems and Political Choices 40
  Concluding Remarks: Clarifying Standards 48
  Notes and References 49

Part Two

KEY AREAS IN THE PURSUIT OF QUALITY IN SCHOOLS AND SCHOOL SYSTEMS

Chapter 4. THE CURRICULUM: PLANNING, IMPLEMENTATION, AND EVALUATION 55

  Concepts and Definitions 55
  Core Curriculum 57
  Curriculum Content 59
  Objectives and Evaluation 62
  Conclusions: Curriculum Planning to Raise Quality 67
  Notes and References 69

Chapter 5. THE VITAL ROLE OF TEACHERS 71

  Teachers and Quality 71
  Attracting Good Recruits 72
  Preparing Effective Teachers 74
  Maintaining Teacher Competence 76
  The Changing Role of Teachers:
    Morale and Motivation 80
  Conclusions 81
  Notes and References 82

Chapter 6. SCHOOL ORGANISATION 85

  Introduction 85
  Cycles of Schooling and Articulation between Levels 86
  Size and Pupil/Teacher Ratios 87
  Time on Task 88
  The School Day and Year 90
  Leadership and Management: Structures and Styles 92
  Information Technologies in Schools and Classrooms 96
  Notes and References 97

Chapter 7. ASSESSMENT, APPRAISAL AND MONITORING 101

  The Need for Assessment 101
  The Appraisal of Teachers 103
  School-based Evaluation 105
  Parental Choice 106
  Evaluation of the Whole System 109
  Notes and References 112

Chapter 8. THE RESOURCES DIMENSION 113

  Quantity and Quality Interactions 113
  Appropriate Physical Resources 117
  Notes and References 123

Chapter 9. THE SCHOOL AS THE HEART OF THE MATTER ... 125

Part Three
SUMMARY AND CONCLUSIONS

Quality: The New Priority	133
Reasons for Concern about School Quality	133
Different Approaches to Quality	135
Key Areas in the Pursuit of Quality in Schools and Systems	137
The School as the Heart of the Matter	141

INTRODUCTION

There is now widespread discussion in OECD Member countries of the need to raise the quality of schooling. The entry of the word "quality" into the lexicon of professional educators, politicians, employers, and the public at large is a new phenomenon though, of course, nouns like "excellence", "standards", and "achievement" have long been common parlance. What it does represent is a fresh emphasis in educational discourse that risks leading to conceptual confusion, if not to facile slogan-making, as it becomes a convenient catch-all response to all the many criticisms currently levelled against public education systems.

Its sudden emergence on the national and international scene did not account alone, however, for OECD's decision to analyse and clarify its significance for educational thinking and practice. In fact, OECD's interest in the issue of quality arose from previous work, as illustrated by the final sentences of the report *Compulsory Schooling in a Changing World*[1], which was the outcome of a comprehensive enquiry spread over four years:

> "The burden of this report is that *the priority for the next ten years will be improvement of the quality of compulsory schooling*. All OECD countries have made tremendous economic efforts during the past twenty years to invest in the material provision of schools and to carry out sweeping structural, organisational and curricular reforms. These efforts have brought considerable success. So far, however, success has been measured largely in material terms. The next phase will call for emphasis on less tangible improvements which will necessarily prove more difficult to achieve than the fulfilment of quantitative targets. It will require education authorities at all levels to consider now what compulsory schooling should look like in ten or twenty years' time. What will society then be wanting from the schools and what will schools be wanting from society?" (p. 145).

The phrasing of that conclusion is important and serves as a basis for the rest of this report. The pursuit of quality in education cannot be treated as a short-term, one-off exercise. It is a permanent priority. Education is not an assembly-line process of mechanically increasing inputs and raising productivity. How to improve its quality raises fundamental questions about societal aims, the nature of participation in decision-making at all levels, and the very purposes of the school as an institution.

The report on compulsory schooling also offered a positive interpretation of recent educational history that can serve as a guide towards qualitative improvement. It affirmed that the educational reforms of post-war years represent a major achievement and that the material efforts expended have brought "considerable success". Yet today there remains widespread questioning of what schools are doing and a corresponding need for clear ideas about how to bring about improvement.

At the very beginning of the present enquiry, confirmation that "quality" was a new priority among educators and politicians was demonstrated by the lively interest aroused by a specially-convened international conference, held in Washington, D.C. in May 1984, which was jointly sponsored by the OECD and the United States federal authorities[2]. Subsequently, when the Ministers of Education of OECD countries met in Paris in 1984, "Quality in Basic Schooling" figured as one of three major items on their agenda. The Ministers concluded their deliberations by issuing a communiqué in which they declared that a priority for future OECD work in the education field should be:

> "*The quality of basic schooling*, particularly basic education related to modern needs in increasingly pluralistic societies, including matters such as: better preparation for adult life; measures to improve the status, effectiveness and professional role of teachers; the organisation, content and structure of the curriculum and methods of evaluation; qualitative factors affecting the performance of schools, including school-based leadership; and programmes designed for the disadvantaged and the handicapped".[3]

Here the term "basic schooling" was meant to comprehend not only essential skills but the broad education that all young people require in order to be given a good start in life. The advice of the Ministers to focus on basic schooling has been followed in this report for it is at this level of the education system that efforts to raise quality are most pronounced. It is recognised, of course, that what happens to children at the primary and secondary levels is crucially influenced by whatever experience they have had of pre-schooling, and by the demands and constraints of the higher levels of education and training that come after. Moreover, basic schooling cannot be treated as an isolated experience in each person's lifetime. The school years are the most formalised and most formative part of the larger whole of lifelong learning and recurrent education, but they are still only a part. Nevertheless, the present scope has been limited to that level of education where public interest and criticisms have concentrated, namely, initial schooling.

Following the Ministerial meeting in November 1984, the work on Quality was pursued in part through a series of international conferences on key topics. These were: *Core Curriculum and Core Skills* held in November 1985[4]; *School Leadership* in January 1986[5]; *Quality in Education: The Vital Role of Teachers* jointly organised with the Italian authorities and held in Rome in May 1986[6]; *Evaluation and Monitoring of the School System* in September 1986[7]. The results of these conferences, and the background material prepared for each, particularly those on the curriculum, teachers, and evaluation, have been closely reflected in the relevant chapters of this report.

Yet, as the list of relevant areas of concern listed by the Ministers of Education in their communiqué shows, the pursuit of quality may be so broadly interpreted as to implicate potentially all analyses and activities concerned with the functioning of schools and the implementation of educational policies. Some limitation of scope is therefore required in order to give a working focus. To arrive at this, two fundamental and related questions have been confronted as they must in any in-depth discussion of the concept of quality in education:

— First, is a prerequisite to any consideration of "quality", including this report, a single definition that then stands both to define the scope and subject matter, and to provide the criteria by which current educational policies and practices should be assessed?

— Second, is clarification of the concept of quality in education meaningful without undertaking an assessment of all aspects of schools and school systems? Apart from the feasibility of doing this, can all OECD countries be assessed collectively with a view to suggesting universal remedies and reform strategies?

The answer to these questions that determined the approach of this report is "no". Despite the need for focus, a single, tight definition of "quality" would require making two questionable assumptions: first, that underlying the complexity of education systems is a set of relatively clear and unconflicting goals that provide the measure of whether quality is being achieved; second, that it should be possible to apply these goals across OECD countries despite their widely diverse traditions and cultures and the variety of conditions prevailing even within national frontiers. It would also entail assuming that educational improvement is to be achieved through a standard model or plan that can then be implemented in a "top-down" fashion. The difficulty of drawing a strict line between those policies specifically inspired by the aim of raising quality and more general school policies explains the selective choice of subjects for the chapters in Part Two.

To question the value of proposing an OECD definition is not to suggest that all definitions of quality are invalid. Manifestos on "quality" based on given definitions can help to fuel the educational debate in each country. But in view of the international dimension of this exercise, a more detached perspective was judged necessary that recognised, as the point of departure, the *variety* of interpretations of quality as well as the range of conditions existing in the different OECD countries. Similarly, in addressing the question "can quality be discussed without engaging in an overall assessment of all educational (in this instance, school) policy and practice?", this report has adopted a restrained aim: to analyse differing interpretations of quality, and the variety of factors that have led to new questions emerging in OECD countries, in the light of international experience, as well as to examine a number of the policy choices commonly seen to be most pertinent to the pursuit of quality in schools.

This modesty of ambition and the salience of the international dimension of the exercise suggest caution too in the use of national research findings. The body of educational research worldwide is already vast and constantly growing. An international report on quality cannot aspire to be a synthesis of this corpus of knowledge, seeking to provide policy-makers with *the* right answers, and this for several reasons apart from purely practical ones. Research certainly informs the debate but it cannot be distilled to provide definitive answers, particularly not applicable to all OECD countries. Findings often conflict. The very specificity of most research severely limits the degree to which the conclusions derived therefrom can be generalised. All studies are necessarily partial, holding constant an array of "outside" factors that in reality impinge on and influence actual processes and outcomes. Even more important than these technical considerations is the fact that no findings are value-free. Values shape not only the style of an enquiry and the questions posed but any given conclusion or set of conclusions can be used to "justify" very different viewpoints. This could scarcely be better illustrated in the educational field than in the very areas under consideration in this report. Research evidence repeatedly enters the political arena purporting unshakably to support opposing views on such questions as "are standards falling?", "does additional expenditure improve outcomes?" and even "do schools make a difference?". Values are right at the heart of a concept as subjective as quality.

The report is presented in three parts, each with a distinct approach. The first — "Quality: The Concept and the Concern" — is essentially conceptual. It aims to identify the dimensions of and approaches to quality, and to raise the problems and dilemmas that these pose. The second — "Key Areas in the Pursuit of Quality in Schools and School Systems" — is concerned with particular policies and practices, drawing, where possible, on concrete evidence and examples. The two parts thus represent contrasting but complementary approaches to the understanding of quality: one concerned with analysis of the concept in the light of current developments in OECD countries, the other addressing the policies and practices that are relevant to the policy-maker and educationist seeking to improve schooling. Based on both of these, the report draws out in Part Three a summary of the main findings and conclusions.

NOTES AND REFERENCES

1. OECD (1983), *Compulsory Schooling in a Changing World*, Paris.
2. A summary record of the meeting is contained in the report "Quality in Education" [ED/MIN(84)5] distributed as one of the principal background documents for the Education Committee meeting at Ministerial Level, 20th-21st November, 1984.
3. OECD (1985), "OECD Ministers Discuss Education in Modern Society", Paris, p. 48 (document for general distribution).
4. The results of the conference have been incorporated into the publication reporting the findings of the special activity on Core Skills, undertaken jointly with the United Kingdom Manpower Services Commission. See Skilbeck, M., Tate, K., and Lowe, N. (forthcoming), *Core Skills and the Curriculum*, OECD, Paris.
5. The conference conclusions have been incorporated in a CERI publication as part of the International School Improvement Project (ISIP) — Stegö, N.E., Gielen, K., Glatter, R., Hord, S.M. (eds.) (1987), *The Role of School Leaders in School Improvement*, OECD/CERI and ACCO, Leuven. See also Hopes, C. (ed.) (1986), *The School and School Improvement*, ACCO, Leuven.
6. The summary record of the meeting is contained in "Quality in Education: The Vital Role of Teachers" (OECD working document, 1986).
7. The summary record of the meeting is contained in "Quality in Education: Evaluation and Monitoring of the School System" (OECD working document, 1986).

Part one

QUALITY: THE CONCEPT AND THE CONCERN

Chapter 1

REASONS FOR THE CURRENT INTEREST IN QUALITY

INTRODUCTION

There is today in OECD countries unprecedented interest in the very quality of schooling. Beginning this report by presenting reasons for this may seem to beg the obvious question "what is quality?", but the context and background of present concerns provide a natural introduction to the more profound analysis of the concept itself that follows in the next chapter. In reality, "quality" means different things to different observers and interest groups; not all share the same perceptions of priorities for change. Only in a few countries or among distinct sections of populations is there so deep a malaise about the functioning of school systems as to lead the perennial quest for incremental improvement to be overtaken by root and branch questioning of how schools perform, though the level of public criticism of schools is, arguably, without precedent. Despite the prominence of the debate in the United States and other Anglo-Saxon countries, there is a junction of factors in evidence in many OECD countries now that help explain why the term "quality" and interest in the qualitative dimension of schooling have come to the fore, even if they are translated differently in the educational policies and practices of each.

REACTIONS TO THE ERA OF GROWTH

At the risk of caricaturing history by oversimplifying the contrasts between one period and the next, there can be no doubt that today the period of the 1960s and early 1970s exercises a profound influence on perceptions of and the shape of education systems. That was a period of unparalleled growth in expenditures and enrolments. Far-reaching structural reforms of schools were initiated in many countries. There was a strong conviction that education was a positive good — for an individual, the route to social mobility; for society, the motor of prosperity[1]. If perceiving the roots of one era in the one that went before has any validity, then that of the 1960s was itself a reaction to the 1940s and 1950s — years of reconstruction from the miseries of pre-war depression and war-time stress. The optimism of the immediate post-war years intensified as more wanted to enjoy the fruits of increasing affluence. Education appeared to be the most obvious means of acquiring it. Predictions were commonplace that industrialised societies were already becoming "post-industrialised," dependent not so much on the production of goods as on the production of knowledge.

Coincidentally, the birth-rate was rising sharply and schools were filled to overflowing. The overriding problem for many education authorities was simply how to build enough new schools and find enough teachers to staff them. Expansion was both demographically and socially impelled, underpinned by the economic rationale that educational growth was a key determinant of the generation of wealth.

The seeds of later discontent, and ultimately of the present concern about quality, were thus sown. OECD economies faltered in the 1970s in the wake of the first oil-price shock. Unemployment levels rose sharply, initially hitting hardest the young and only later giving rise to the widespread phenomenon of long-term unemployment among all age groups. Not only had the simple formula "more education, more prosperity" been found wanting, but the severe difficulties young people experienced in entering the labour market at all caused some people to blame schools for failing to prepare them adequately for working life. The link between education and social mobility no longer appeared self-evident.

As public expenditures on education ceased to increase or even diminished, and as other sectors of government became fiercely competitive for scarce resources, the sheer size and expense of education systems fell under scrutiny — how efficient were they? did they give value for money? Just as demographic and expenditure growth had gone hand-in-hand in the 1950s and 1960s, so the economic downturn coincided with a declining birth-rate and falling school rolls. With the hunt for new teachers to staff schools no longer a priority, the spotlight could begin to focus on the performance of the teachers already employed and those few being newly recruited. Had rapid expansion brought in its train too many teachers, ill-suited or ill-prepared for the onerous task of educating the next generation, who would nevertheless remain in service for many years to come? Many critics so pronounced.

With the mood switching to caution, even to pessimism, there was a perceptible shift in dominant ideologies. The international sway of egalitarian precepts, regarding the State as principally responsible for ensuring an equitable distribution of goods and services[2], began to yield to more conservative ideas of how societies should function that predicated less active governmental intervention and more reliance on the principles of the market economy and individual self-help as the mechanisms for social organisation and distribution. In the international exchange of ideas about education among Western industrialised nations, where once the Swedish experience had set the model example, other countries became equally influential voices.

Like any brief history, these paragraphs present an oversimplification. They telescope complex social and economic developments into neat categories and exaggerate the degree of contrast. One example of this is the fact that educational growth far from ceased since the early 1970s — the pre-primary sector continued to expand in many countries and a whole array of post-compulsory offerings in education and training were introduced, not least as a response to the employment difficulties of the young. Nor should the fact of rapid educational expansion be seen to imply that it was purely "growth at all costs" while merely supplying more of the same, for there was a rich creation of new programmes and pedagogies in the 1960s and early 1970s and, contrariwise, some people were already questioning then the quality of at least a part of the rapidly expanded provision. Nor were changing social perceptions about education necessarily supported by the evidence. The link between educational success and social mobility became, if anything, more firmly established as unemployment levels rose; it was the labour market opportunities themselves that were becoming scarcer. And, of course, all countries did not share identical experiences. Nevertheless, when all the caveats have been entered, the two dominant features of the earlier period — expansion (*quantitative growth*) and the widening of educational access to new clienteles (greater *equality of opportunity*) — provide a natural backcloth to the shift of emphasis towards *quality*, though, as argued throughout the report, the concepts of quality, quantity, and equality are inextricably intertwined.

Yet, it is likely that a sharp, or at least sharper, public scrutiny of education would have eventually taken place irrespective of the economic reversals of the 1970s. Sooner or later, it was highly likely that a call would be made to assess the impact of wide-ranging structural reforms and the degree to which ambitious goals had been met in reality. It was only to be expected that greater accountability would become the order of the day when such large public resources were being devoted to, and so many people being occupied by, modern education systems. In addition, new challenges and problems appeared in the 1980s. Reactions to the 1960s did not herald a return to the 1950s. The debate about quality, in other words, is not simply a dialogue with the recent past.

SCHOOLS AND TEACHERS IN QUESTION

One important reason behind the current concern about quality is, therefore, disappointment with the ability of organisational and structural reforms to solve outstanding educational problems. Institutional arrangements have been modified time and again, yet large numbers of pupils still reach the end of their schooling with patently low attainment levels and no enthusiasm for learning. Educationally, at least two aspects can be distinguished: system-wide change does not necessarily alter organisational practice at the school level; organisational reform is but one ingredient of revitalising teaching and learning in schools. Many more pupils leave school now than before with some form of qualification but the dissatisfaction of employers has not abated. The egalitarian is as likely to complain as the conservative that young people are being sold short by an unresponsive and essentially traditionalist system. With hindsight, it has become clear that the heady aspiration that some held out in the 1960s to bring about sweeping societal changes through educational reorganisation alone was never likely to be realised given that the societies and economies in which schools are placed have remained essentially unequal and imperfect.

With a more circumspect vision of what schools can achieve by themselves, part of the concern about quality, therefore, stems from the repeated lesson that altering the main structural and organisational forms of schooling does not necessarily lead to a change in content and processes. On the surface, this might appear to lead to a narrowing of focus on to school variables and a retreat from the loftier ambitions of earlier years. In fact, the challenges are if anything greater — institutions can be reorganised through legislative fiat; it is far more difficult to change pedagogical practices and to bring about the active involvement of all students in the teaching/learning process.

Education practices are in fact remarkably stable over time despite repeated reforms. The classroom, and, within it, the "recitation" mode, continue to dominate. Goodlad reports the stark figure that of 150 minutes of classroom talk, only an average of 7 minutes is initiated by students themselves[3]. Other findings from the United States[4], and from Sweden, Germany, Finland, Belgium, and Portugal arrive at the same conclusion[5] and suggest that this pattern has been typical over at least the last half century if not longer. To take another example, a growing body of research shows how persistent are the differences in teacher time and attention devoted to boys, on the one hand, and to girls, on the other, that even teachers determined to treat the sexes equally find hard to change[6]. More generally, whatever the institutional organisation of schools, established patterns of differentiation stubbornly persist, either overtly through banding and streaming or covertly through the "hidden curriculum". As expressed in a recent OECD report:

> "It might be inferred that a sharp polarisation exists between countries that have opted to retain selection and those that have opted for the common school. In fact, the crux is how much differentiation occurs within individual schools and when it begins. In practice, common schools vary considerably in the way they distribute pupils and groups and apply the curriculum".[7]

The purpose of raising these examples is not to discuss why particular pedagogical practices are so entrenched or what forms differentiation ought to take but to suggest that a major reason for interest in the quality of schooling derives from the necessity of delving more profoundly into what Goodlad has called "a place called school"[8].

Even if the general perception of the need to focus more closely on schools has thus increased over the years, the above considerations would apply at any time and so do not in themselves explain current preoccupations with what goes on inside schools. In other significant respects, however, schools are confronted today with challenges and problems that are peculiarly contemporary and that argue for reappraisal of their basic purposes and their performance. Perhaps the most obvious is the sheer size and complexity of school systems in the 1980s. The minimum leaving age has been gradually or, in some cases, dramatically extended from 12, 13, or 14 years in the post-war years, to 15, and is now commonly 16 years. In several countries, post-compulsory education has become so much the norm that the end of compulsory schooling is *de facto* losing its significance as the major watershed in students' careers. There are flourishing initiatives at the post-compulsory level, many outside the formal system but in which schools are often expected to participate actively — themselves providing a challenge to long-established habits — but the formal upper secondary school or college remains the principal destination for young people above the minimum leaving age in the majority of OECD countries and this route is becoming more pronounced in several.

The net result of all this is that schools are now having to cope with a perplexing breadth of talent and motivation among their students. Many of these find the traditional academic meal, even with more choice of dishes, distinctly unappetising. Thus, a major problem facing schools today is the sizeable minority of students who are poorly motivated and plainly bored. The questions arising for policy are painfully difficult to resolve. Can countries maintain the basic principle that all young people should be introduced to a common culture and allowed equal access to the higher, more academic reaches of their education systems? How far can the authorities go in introducing diversity of approaches and programmes before opportunities become unacceptably unequal? Can the growing pressures to keep young people ever longer within the confines of schools and colleges be accommodated without either jeopardising the academic ambitions of the more scholastic or failing to provide a meaningful diet of learning for the less academically-inclined? Whether or not the terminology of "quality" is applied, these questions call for a profound reappraisal of the purposes and practice of schooling.

Teachers find themselves in the firing line of these new pressures and challenges and are variously criticised for obstructing change, being ill-informed about the world outside schools, or for failing to uphold the traditions of the magisterial instructor. In many countries, they are suffering from a crisis of professional identity, receiving conflicting messages about how they should approach their work. Darling-Hammond et al.[9] have identified four quite distinct conceptions of what is expected of them:

- *teaching as labour*: the activities of the teacher should be rationally planned, and programmatically organised by administrators, with the teacher merely responsible for carrying out the instructional programme;
- *teaching as craft*: teaching is seen in this conception as requiring a répertoire of specialised techniques and as well as mastering the techniques, the teacher must acquire general rules for their application;
- *teaching as profession*: the teacher needs not only a répertoire of specialised techniques but also the ability to exercise judgement about when these techniques should be applied and hence a body of theoretical knowledge;
- *teaching as art*: based not only on professional knowledge and skills but on a set of personal resources uniquely defined; techniques and their application may be novel, unconventional, and unpredictable[10].

At the same time, each new initiative that schools are expected to implement — familiarisation of pupils with micro-technologies, development of multicultural programmes, gender equality policies, mainstreaming the handicapped, designing work experience schemes, as well as developing new curricula and methods of school-based assessment and introducing pupil records — depends for its success on the efforts and commitment of teachers. With severe curtailment of teacher recruitment in most countries and the limited utility of initial training for equipping teachers for the many tasks listed above, it is not surprising that teachers complain of being overstretched. In some countries, they are concerned that their social status has fallen and their material rewards have declined just as the professional demands upon them have become heavier than ever before. Too often, they have to teach in poorly equipped and maintained buildings, suffering the effects of expenditure cutbacks and the legacy of an influential research tradition that was purported to show that additional resources "make no difference" to educational outcomes.

While teachers express worries about their capacity to deliver an education of quality, there is in many countries official disquiet about the professional and personal qualifications of new entrants to the teaching force. Fears are voiced that talented graduates are not entering the profession and that accomplished practising teachers are seeking other jobs. Yet as the typology of conceptions of teaching roles and duties outlined above helps illustrate, it is rarely clear exactly who the "good" teacher is supposed to be and what is expected of her or him. He or she is unlikely to be simply the graduate with at least reasonable grades from college. Just as the basic purposes and functions of schools require fundamental reappraisal in the light of current expectations and capacity, so is corresponding clarification needed of the professional duties of teachers.

QUALITY IN EDUCATION AND ECONOMIC IMPERATIVES

Two economic reasons behind the concern about quality in education have already been referred to in this chapter: first, unprecedentedly high levels of youth unemployment inspired the charge that youngsters were being inadequately equipped for the world of work, an educational "explanation" of unemployment that lost some of its force as the unemployment phenomenon spread to all sections of the active population; second, the disruption of uninterrupted economic growth challenged the simplistic quantitative formula of "more education, more prosperity". As education had flourished in the 1960s when it had a relatively clear economic rationale, so its public standing declined in the 1970s when that rationale came under question as its fortunes faltered.

By the latter years of the 1980s, the fashion has changed once more. Acknowledgement of the importance of "human capital" in economic development has re-emerged and with it renewed priority for education and training. The recent recovery is one factor of explanation but recognition of the importance of technological innovation and the speed of economic change are probably of more direct significance. When OECD Labour Market Ministers met in Paris in November 1986, they considered in one of their background reports the following argument:

> "Rather than dramatically reducing the need for labour, technological innovation has transformed much of the qualitative demand for labour, as innovations have led to changes in occupation, the organisation of work, and ultimately, in the skills required for employment. Qualified manpower has come to be viewed as a prerequisite to realising the full economic advantage of technological innovations and, as such, at least a partial determinant of how quickly new technologies are diffused. Technology-linked changes in the workplace are also feeding fears of an adult 'job literacy' or 'functional literacy' problem. This is also occurring as low-wage unskilled jobs disappear and the rising threshold of minimum competency required for employment overtakes the qualifications of experienced adults who entered the labour market several years ago. Finally, the need for economies to adjust to a full range of other structural changes — beyond the technological — and uncertainty about future changes has increased the need for labour market flexibility so as to allow a critical margin for adjustment."[11]

If "human capital" theories and formulations are once more respectable and, as a result, there is a powerful economic reason to support education, the emphasis has markedly changed from twenty years ago. As the above quotation reveals, greater attention is now paid to the *qualitative* demand for labour, and hence to the qualities possessed by the labour force rather than to purely quantitative expansion. The speed and ubiquity of technological innovation postulate a demand for workers capable of adapting flexibly to new demands by mastering knowledge and skills that facilitate occupational change and by acquiring the breadth of expertise to be able to discharge a variety of tasks in work organised into teams[12]. Some take the even stronger line of asserting that what determines healthy economic performance in OECD countries today compared with earlier years is the ability to produce high-quality goods and services thanks to a workforce which has correspondingly high-quality knowledge and skills. In sum, there is a variety of powerful economic and technological arguments behind the current interest in the quality of education.

But if a good general case can thus be elaborated, it is less clear what the implications are for schools. A crucial difference between the current generation of arguments about the economic benefits of education and those of the sixties is that considerably more weight is given now to recurrent education and training for *adults*. There is also greater emphasis on *non-formal* provision, both as a fact and as a desirable source of flexibility, but which is outside the school and college system and beyond the immediate control of education authorities. Rapid change of technologies and work processes suggests that the knowledge and skills that each will apply throughout working life will also be changing — the specifics learned at school are thus threatened by impending obsolescence. Moreover, there is the unresolved debate about how many of the workforce will be affected by the demands for high-level, flexible knowledge and skills, requiring continual up-dating and renewal. Posing the question in terms of global "upskilling" versus "deskilling" in the labour force may be too simplistic, but it is difficult to argue that all, or even the large majority, of the future workers at present in school will be in the high-skill job sectors. Many, indeed, may suffer protracted periods of unemployment. Unlike those who assert a simple, direct link between economic performance and educational quality, therefore, we see the implications of these arguments for basic schooling to be less than straightforward.

The relevant point to be made here is that along with the renewed salience accorded to education for economic reasons, and with greater attention being paid to "quality", has come heightened awareness of the complexities involved. Many of the arguments supporting that enhanced salience address principally sectors of education and training outside the school system itself. It is much easier to assert that schooling should not be "more of the same" than it is to state with confidence what specified content should be increased.

There are certain grounds for being wary about embracing uncritically new economic rationales. The social and cultural missions of schooling remain as important as ever — schools do not exist exclusively to lubricate the economy. Economic and political pressures tend to be immediate whereas education's contribution to society and the economy tends to be over the long term. Sceptics might argue (with some justification on the basis of past evidence) that it is customary to resort to educational solutions to social and economic ills whenever other policies have failed, and this is surely an insecure foundation on which to establish educational reform. It also risks public disenchantment when promised results are not immediately forthcoming. Sceptics might also argue that the political change of climate is more one of reluctant acceptance of the inevitability of resorting to educational responses to the seemingly permanent feature of high levels of youth unemployment in some OECD countries than an active belief in the potential of education to contribute to economic growth. In other words, it is important to separate carefully rhetoric from reality and to be clear about precisely what economic objectives *do* imply for education in general, and schooling in particular. This is not to say that the economic and political pressure for raising educational quality should be resisted; on the contrary, it represents an opportunity to be seized. It should be understood, however, that the optimum contribution of schools will necessarily be long-term and will often operate indirectly rather than be evident and direct.

There is, in some quarters, a further economic incentive behind the current interest in educational quality. Fears have been expressed in some countries, notably in the United States, France, and the United Kingdom, that unless schools are improved, their countries will further lose their competitive edge in the world economy. The phenomenon of international competition giving rise to internal dissection of the way school systems function is not new. A well-known landmark in the post-war educational history of the United States, for example, was the "Sputnik crisis" in the late 1950s. The technical advances made by the Eastern-bloc countries at that time led to dire warnings that without major improvements in schooling, the United States would be overtaken by its great rival. The equivalent arguments today are fuelled by enquiries into cross-country educational attainment (notably by the International Association for the Evaluation of Educational Achievement [IEA]), the results of which become political ammunition mainly when unfavourable comparisons are made in international league tables. The targets of the worry tend to be twofold — immediate rivals among the highly industrialised Western countries and the rapidly emerging competitors in South East Asia and Latin America. The worries in the latter case stem not only from the shifting patterns of world trade but also from the results of international assessments showing that certain rapidly developing countries in South East Asia, with class sizes considerably larger than those in most OECD education systems and with students living in a social milieu notably less privileged, are now scoring as well or sometimes even better than students in the rich industrialised ones, especially in mathematics and the sciences[13]. There may be a certain irony in the fact that greater internationalisation of outlook has induced the educational equivalent of national protectionism but it is not surprising that such comparisons induce the call for enquiry into why the imbalance has occurred and whether there are lessons to be drawn.

THE SOCIAL CONTEXT OF SCHOOLS

Just as there has been a revival in favour of the economic rationale for education, and with it greater focus on qualitative factors, so has there been a corresponding revival of interest in the social value of schooling and with it reaffirmation of what had always accorded with common sense, namely that schools do "make a difference" and that "good" schools, variously defined, are better for children than "bad" ones. Arguments have hinged around whether schools exercise an autonomous influence on student achievement, over and above the powerful factors of home background and community. Well-known sociological studies in the 1960s and 1970s had appeared to question that this autonomous influence existed and, in so doing, had undermined not only the egalitarian ambitions of school reform but challenged the very value of schooling itself.

The sway of this sociological pessimism has now receded and the atmosphere today is once more supportive of efforts to improve individual schools. Given the particular prominence that American research has enjoyed, it is interesting to observe these shifts in that country, and to note the views of Marshall Smith (himself a co-author of the famous Jencks study) who summarised these shifts of opinion in an OECD report thus:

"The *Equality of Educational Opportunity* report by Coleman, and Jencks *et al. Inequality* fanned a debate about the relative effects of schools and family background and home experience. To sociologists, the low percentages of variance explained by differences among schools indicated the lack of effect that schools might have. To economists, the percentages of variance explained were less important than the coefficients which suggested that there were major differences between the lowest and highest achieving schools, even after home background was controlled. To reformers, none of the debate made much sense since the data only reflected what existed, not what might exist. All agreed that the family background and experience of children are important. All also agreed that there was lots of variation within schools and that the psychologists should work on this. The general resolution with respect to the potential effects of schools is more on the side of the economists and reformers. Coleman, in a recent report on public and private schools, makes the current argument that variations in schools can make a significant difference."[14]

These arguments turn on the relative weight of social and school influences on *individual* students. In fact, research such as Coleman's 1966 study and the Jencks *et al.* 1972 report never claimed that schools as such made "no difference". What they could not detect in their evidence were signs of significant effects from *differences* in schools and school variables. Part of the reason for this may well have been that this research tradition failed to formulate its school variables closely and precisely enough. More recent studies of schools have been much more attentive to the detailed realities of process and practice. In other words, they have been more concerned with the qualitative, "micro" realities of classrooms and schools as lying at "the heart of the matter" — the title of Chapter 9.

More general features of change that affect the climate and context in which schools operate may be no less relevant to social concerns about quality. Much of the disquiet expressed about young people's attitudes and behaviour in fact refers to a much broader range of factors than simply the learning that takes place within classroom walls. Such a comprehensive perspective is all too often absent. The school is the obvious target of criticism when it does occur since it is the institution that has acquired extensive public responsibility for the care and socialisation of the young, often willingly, in areas that before belonged to families, churches, and communities. Having been given or assumed this responsibility, however, schools are now beset by conflicting pressures — to demonstrate that they have adequately fulfilled the extensive socialisation tasks that they have acquired, on the one hand, and to adapt to the changing external environment that is tending to encroach on their traditional "enclosed" status, on the other. More is expected of them even as their freedom is increasingly cramped. Searching questions thus come to be asked about what schools do and, indeed, whether they are "any good".

An interesting example of the tensions that this imposes on schools arises from the undoubted influence exercised today by the media. Even if unambiguous and neutral conclusions from research on the media's influence are scarce, the many hours young people typically spend watching television, for example, cannot but affect their thinking, behaviour, and attitudes. The types of knowledge and images received are different from those which the teacher seeks to convey in the classroom. Though some is undoubtedly beneficial, one effect is to reduce the utility of the written word and the perceived value of reading relative to visual stimuli. Television viewing is also a passive activity in contrast with the active pursuit of hobbies or play. Television opens up the adult world in direct, if intangible, ways that affect children's attitudes towards authority and the childhood environment. Some critics also express concern about the detrimental impact on learning at school of the fatigue induced by late-night viewing. Television and other media are now a reality of modern life but their spread has occurred rapidly and pervasively, with little conscious societal thinking about their overall impact. The point to be made here is that schools cannot reasonably be held accountable for parental habits of television-viewing, reading, and extra-school activities. And yet teachers and schools find themselves victims of the privileged status they have acquired in bringing up successive generations of the young since doubts about the suitability of that upbringing are inevitably directed against schools even when the criticisms fasten on perceived shortcomings whose causes extend well beyond classroom walls.

Given the very high proportions of parents now working in OECD countries, the social pressures remain firmly on schools to maintain their primary responsibility for child care and socialising the young. Still more is this true as growing numbers of children are being raised in single-parent families[15]. But the enclosed, comfortable world of the school is no longer typical, if it ever was. Parents in general are better educated than in the past, often up to levels equal with or higher than their own children's teachers. Adults can regard themselves as educational experts on the basis of their personal experiences of school. Deferential attitudes to adult authority are less evident, as young people have high expectations but uncertain futures, frequently rendering discipline problematic. The rapid spread of microtechnologies in many homes often makes children more expert in their use than their teachers. The "explosion of knowledge" sharply raises questions about the legitimacy of what is actually transmitted in school curricula. As a result, teachers cannot rest their authority on their special status as founts of wisdom. Education authorities are uncertain of what parts of the exponentially growing corpus of knowledge are appropriate for the young and of how to choose between reflecting its breadth through offering a superficial introduction or giving concentrating attention to diminishing aspects of the whole.

Expectations and reality are often at odds, with teachers and schools at the centre when tensions arise. Many politicians and parents use memories of their own schooling as their reference points and these are no longer realistic in a world of rapid technological development and changing attitudes to authority. Teachers may regard themselves as autonomous professionals with subject expertise, but their view is increasingly threatened by competing sources of knowledge in societies where everyone can claim to be an educational expert. Young people have been raised in relative affluence with the message that education is essential for future success only to discover that the openings actually available are severely limited. Tensions arise not only because aims and conditions are changing and are often in conflict but because the expectations of schools are now higher than ever. Recipes for returning to the "good old days" are pleas for a world where all knew their place and expectations were limited. They are, accordingly, simply unrealistic.

All the changes briefly sketched here render the schools' purposes and tasks uncertain at the same time as they increase the pressures for greater *accountability*. These pressures stem in part from factors already mentioned — education has grown into a very large, expensive public sector and, with recession and unemployment, the competition for the scarcer benefits to be gained through educational success has intensified. They also result from external forces breaching the walled domain of the school. The more outside interests become deeply implicated in the running of schools, the greater is the demand for tangible signs and indicators to be produced of what happens within school classrooms. The educational debate in some countries is thus preoccupied with assessment and outcomes, that is, with quality control. Particular sections of the community have also developed articulate claims on schools, not just in order to have readier access to the available provision but to have a larger say in the making of educational policy both in terms of the determination of priorities and in the shaping of the curricular content.

CONCLUDING REMARKS

In a number of OECD countries, education has become markedly "politicised". There is no longer a clear social consensus about goals. Educational decision-making has risen to the forefront of national politics in a number of OECD countries. Convenient ideological labels such as "left" and "right", "conservative" and "progressive", "elitist" and "egalitarian" no longer describe adequately the complex clusterings of values and claims now impinging on schools. The term "malaise" is now commonly evoked to describe the state of schools in some countries.

The clarification of aims and objectives, and choice of coherent means of realising them, have thus become high priorities. That process of clarification to be sustained over time must essentially be a societal concern and takes place within countries, albeit drawing upon international understanding and evidence. International reports such as this one cannot be a substitute for that process.

As and when it occurs, societal questioning of the appropriate aims and setting for the upbringing of children may well prove to be a painful exercise. A plethora of duties has been grafted on an institution — the school — whose roots lie in the establishment of national education systems in the 19th century under strikingly different conditions. Any interrogation of what is expected of schools must include questioning of the very validity of their institutional form in the light of contemporary needs. Yet the onus is on the critics who view schools as largely inflexible institutions, caught in bureaucratic webs and ill adapted to modern society, to propose realistic, concrete alternatives. For it is scarcely conceivable that the upbringing of the young will not continue to be entrusted to a specialised agency or agencies for learning and socialisation. Schools, in some form, are here to stay.

NOTES AND REFERENCES

1. An early international expression of this optimism was the OECD Conference on *Economic Growth and Investment in Education* held in Washington, D.C. in October 1961 (proceedings published in 1962).
2. See OECD (1981), *The Welfare State in Crisis*, Paris.
3. Goodlad, J. (1982), "A Study of Schooling: Some Implications for School Improvement", *Phi Delta Kappan*, Vol. 64.
4. Hoetker J. and Ahlbrandt, P.A. Jr. (1969), "The Persistence of Recitation", *American Educational Research Journal*, Vol. 6, No. 2. pp. 145-167.
5. Reported by Lundgren, U. (1987), in *New Challenges for Teachers and their Education*, Standing Conference of European Ministers of Education, Background Report, Council of Europe, Strasbourg. Based on:
   — Gustafsson, C. (1977), *Classroom Interaction*, Stockholm Institute of Education. Studies in curriculum theory and cultural reproduction No. 1, CWK/Gleerup/Liber, Lund.
   — Lundgren, U.P. (1977), *Model Analysis of Pedagogical Processes*, Stockholm Institute of Education. Studies in curriculum theory and cultural reproduction No. 2, CWK/Gleerup/Liber, Lund.
   — De Landsheere, G. and Bayer, G. (1970), *Comment les maîtres enseignent: Analyse des instructions verbales en classe*, Ministère de l'Education Nationale et de la Culture, Documentation No. 21, Brussels.
   — Spanhel, D. (1971), *Die Sprache des Lehrers*, Pädagogischer Verlag Schwann, Düsseldorf.
   — Koskenniemi, M. and Komulainen, E. (1974), *Investigations into the Instructional Process*, Institute of Education, University of Helsinki. Research Bulletin No. 39.
   — Pedro, E. (1981), *Social Stratification and Classroom Discourse*, Stockholm Institute of Education. Studies in curriculum theory and cultural reproduction No. 6, CWK/Gleerup/Liber, Lund.
   — Pedro, E. (1984), *O discurso na aula. Uma análise socio-linguística de prática escolar em Portugal*, Edições Rolim, Lisbon.
6. Discussed in the literature review chapters by Safilios-Rothschild, C., "Sex Differences in Early Socialization and Upbringing and their Consequences for Educational Choices and Outcomes", and by Whyte, J., "The Development of Sex Stereotyped Attitudes Among Boys and Girls: Different Models of their Origins and their Educational Implications", Chapters 2 and 3 in OECD

(1986), *Girls and Women in Education: A Cross-National Study of Sex Inequality in Upbringing in Schools and Colleges*, Paris. See also: Council of Europe (1982), *Sex Stereotyping in Schools*, Council of Europe, Swets and Zeitlinger-Lisse, Strasbourg.

7. OECD (1985), *Education in Modern Society*, Paris. p. 66.
8. Goodlad, J. (1983), *A Place Called School*, McGraw Hill, New York.
9. Darling-Hammond, L., Wise, A.E., and Pease, S.R. (1983), "Teacher Evaluation in the Organizational Context: A Review of the Literature", *Review of Educational Research*, Vol. 53, No. 3. pp. 285-328.
10. Discussed further in Lawton, D. (1986), "The Role and Professional Status of the Teacher: Some Sociological Perspectives" (OECD working document).
11. OECD (1986), "Education and Training for Manpower Development", paper prepared for the meeting of the Manpower and Social Affairs Committee at Ministerial Level 18th and 19th November, 1986, Paris. pp. 1-2 (document on general distribution).
12. Discussed in more detail in OECD (1986), "Education and Structural Adjustment" (OECD working document). See also OECD (1987), *Structural Adjustment and Economic Performance*, Paris, Chapter 1.
13. For a summary presentation of findings from the Second IEA Study see the special issue of *Comparative Education Review*, Vol. 31, No. 1, February 1987.
14. Smith, M.S. (1986), "Education Reform in the United States" (OECD working document). Paper prepared for Joint Italy/OECD Conference on *The Vital Role of Teachers*, Rome, May 6-8, 1986, p. 9. Based on:
    — Coleman, J.S., *et al*. (1966), *Equality of Educational Opportunity*, U.S. Government Printing Office, Washington D.C.
    — Jencks, C., *et al*. (1972), *Inequality: A Reassessment of the Effect of Family and Schooling in America*, Basic Books, New York.
    — Coleman, J.S., Hoffer, T., and Kilgore, S. (1982), *High School Achievement*, Basic Books, New York.
15. See papers prepared for the OECD Conference of National Experts, *Lone Parents: The Economic Challenge of Changing Family Structures*, 15th-17th December, 1987 (ultimately to be published in a single volume).

Chapter 2

THE CONCEPT OF QUALITY

INTRODUCTION

"The 'quality of Australian education' depends on the selection of relevant elements, the assessment of the character of these elements and the weighting given to their relative importance. The assessment of quality is thus complex and value laden. There is no simple uni-dimensional measure of quality. In the same way as the definition of what constitutes high quality education is multi-dimensional, so there is no simple prescription of the ingredients necessary to achieve high quality education; many factors interact — students and their backgrounds; staff and their skills; schools and their structure and ethos; curricula; and societal expectations".
(The Karmel Committee Review Report, 1985)[1].

"The meaning of quality is unclear, and the term is variously used by different interests. Statements, some more precise than others, concerning the quality of education are made in various contexts, but systematic studies on the subject are few and far between. As a result, statements concerning quality are not always well-founded, whatever the sense in which the term is used".
(From the Swedish statement contributed to the OECD activity on Quality, 1984).

Thus do two statements from countries as far apart geographically as Australia and Sweden express the complexity of the quality concept. This report is consistent with these views in that it eschews a single, tight definition of quality. Instead, it will attempt to analyse the dimensions that enter different definitions and interpretations, whether of the notion of "quality" in general, or of its specific applications in the educational field.

QUALITY — THE WORD

"Quality" has a variety of meanings. It can be a descriptive rather than a normative term. It can refer simply to a *trait* or *attribute*. Thus, a pupil or teacher, a school or school district, a regional or national education system, can have any number of qualities or defining characteristics. "Quality" may also be used as a more aggregate or collective term. No longer simply a synonym for an attribute or characteristic, it refers in this sense to *the defining essence* of an entity. It is then more accurate to speak of *the* quality of whatever is being referred to, e.g. a classroom, school, or system. Although one can categorise these meanings of the word as descriptive, they are not uncontentious since different observers and interests may identify as essential quite different defining characteristics. Even so, to talk, for instance, of a school's qualities in these senses need not imply value judgements.

The importance of the term "quality" in the educational context, including its political significance, increases substantially, however, when it is given a normative interpretation. A dictionary will include such definitions of the word as "*degree of excellence*" or "*relative nature or kind or character*". When quality means "degree of excellence", two aspects are encompassed: that of judgements of worth and that of position on an implied scale of good and bad. To judge the quality of a school, for instance, as "poor", "mediocre", or "excellent" means both applying, whether roughly or precisely, a certain notion of merit, and identifying, again more or less approximately, where that school is positioned relative to other schools.

To make matters still more complicated, qualitative *judgements* as described above are rarely made without a concern to effect *improvements*, at least when the result of an assessment has proved less than satisfactory. How best to realise improvements, especially when conflicts and trade-offs are involved, is no less an area of potential controversy than the initial assessment. To give one example, disagreement in the United States is just as palpable concerning what should be done, if anything, in response to the long-term decline in Scholastic Aptitude Test (SAT) scores as it is concerning the facts of the decline itself.

The shades of meaning of the word are not yet exhausted. "Quality" may implicitly denote the *good* or the *excellent* as in phrases such as "the quality teacher" or "the quality school". Though, strictly speaking, it is difficult and even misleading to separate rigidly the qualitative and quantitative, in normal parlance "quality" may also be used in *contradistinction with "quantity"*. Qualitative assessments are, in this sense, those which are made intuitively, because the nature and complexity of the phenomenon observed defy segmentation into measurable parts. Judgements of this kind are made daily in education many times in many settings: "As a parent, I can just go into a school and get a feel for the place and I can tell whether it's any good or not"; "Everyone in the school just knows who are the good teachers and who are the bad ones". School inspection or teacher appraisal will often entail precisely these kinds of qualitative judgements. Although not everyone will agree with them and, although sometimes hasty or ill-informed, they are the stuff of the creative, human enterprise of schooling.

The very term "quality" is thus multi-faceted, and often subjective. Four different uses of the word can be identified:

— Attributes (specific) or defining essence (collective): descriptive;
— Degree of excellence or relative worth: normative;
— The good or excellent: normative;
— Non-quantified traits or judgements: descriptive or normative: (containing elements of the above).

Given these dimensions of the word, it is hardly surprising that assertions about quality in education are often controversial. Individuals and interest groups can and do differ substantially over what they judge, in general, to be good or bad. That education has become increasingly politicised over recent years and that a broad national consensus on goals is often no longer the rule may be seen both as a reason why the concern for quality in schooling has come to the fore and as a major reason why its resolution is so problematic. Individuals and interest groups may be no less at odds in their assessment of where a particular practice or situation comes on the notional scale of good and bad, even assuming broad agreement on what in general constitutes better or worse. Judgements may be made of the most specific entities, e.g. the pupil, teacher, classroom, or practical application of a pedagogical technique, through to the most aggregate appraisal, such as of a national education system. And attitudes to the measurement of "quality" are no less varied.

QUALITY IN SCHOOLING: DIMENSIONS AND APPROACHES

The semantic distinctions thus far identified could be further elaborated and refined but to go beyond a dictionary exercise requires examination of the actual approaches that are the cynosure of educational analysis and debate. Below, dimensions of, and perspectives on, quality are identified and distinguished in terms of their differing focus and emphasis. This is necessarily a selection rather than an exhaustive list simply because of the many-sided, often subjective, open-ended nature of the concept. They are presented as a series of contrasts that are in practice overlapping.

a) **Style of enquiry and level of schooling addressed**

"Quality in schooling" can be a topic of detached educational and sociological analysis or, instead, qualitative issues can be central to the committed aims of interest groups, educationists, and political parties. There is an important difference of approach between, for example, Lundgren's assertion as an academic observer of the prominence of the quality issue that "criticism of education and the concern for the quality of education find their roots in decreasing confidence in education"[2], on the one hand, and the parent who removes his or her child from a school because of dissatisfaction with the classroom teacher or principal, or the teacher protesting about inadequate laboratory facilities, or the political party official drawing up an education manifesto for radical change, on the other. Neither is more "correct". All approaches, whether of scholars, politicians, parents, or teachers, are nevertheless inspired by certain notions of the betterment of schooling, however indirectly.

The focus for improving education can be on very specific and local aspects of schooling through to the education system as a whole. The proposition may seem obvious — which is adopted depends on the "actor" and the goals in question — but this difference needs at least to be stated. The framing of relevant issues will not be the same for, say, a National Commission mandated to assess the overall performance of its country's system and to recommend reforms, and the district inspector or superintendent hired to improve the performance of a notorious pocket of inner-city problem schools. As explained in the Introduction, a major stimulus for the OECD activity that resulted in this report is that new qualitative concerns are widespread at the "macro" national, even international, level and that this is to be distinguished from the perennial "micro" task of organising schools as efficiently and effectively as possible. The line between the two is far from hard-and-fast, however; national systems are, after all, only the aggregate of the schools and school districts that constitute them, and national-level debates would be no more than ephemeral if they did not at least reflect grass-roots realities.

b) **Goals and objectives**

Is the broad criterion by which the quality of a school system is to be assessed the achievement of its goals, and should this include all or only a restricted set of goals? At first sight, the answer to the first part of this question seems obviously to be "yes": the criterion for assessing the quality of a school system should be its aims and goals on the grounds that the nearer it comes to meeting these, the better is the quality of the education that it provides. Although easy to state, however, this answer to the question does not provide in practice ready-made guidelines for improving quality in education for at least three main reasons.

The first reason stems from the factor mentioned in the previous chapter and taken up in more detail in *d)* — "Quality for whom?". In an era of general consensus, little weight would be attached to that question. But in the 1980s, and in those countries in particular where education has come to the forefront of political debate, the question has become perplexing and unavoidable. Should the goals be those of official government policy? Parents? Students? Teachers? Employers? Feminists? Racial minorities? Those of the handicapped? Should it be some amalgam of all of these? Indeed, even each one of these groups does not have a single coherent set of goals, explicitly formulated, and each country has its own political processes through which differing claims are negotiated, to the advantage of some and the disadvantage of others. Of course, goals may be formulated at such a level of generality that few would dissent from them but in that case they will cease to be sufficiently precise to permit appraisal of whether "quality" has improved or deteriorated. Putting all these considerations together, the upshot is scarcely a neat set of guidelines for assessing quality.

The second reason why basing the assessment of quality on the achievement of broad goals is problematic is that they are general statements of desired outcomes that can, as with health or economic well-being, always be better. To realise all goals would be utopian. This means that there is a necessary political, as well as a technical, element in the decision about whether a goal has been satisfactorily realised in practice. In establishing priorities, trade-offs and conflicts among the aims of education must be accommodated; the attainment of more of one desired end will often mean falling short of another. These two reasons together suggest that, contrary to the frequent tenor of debate, standards are not absolute. They are perforce compromises aimed at an optimal balance.

In the absence of absolute standards, Lundgren's position mentioned above suggests one route to the clarification of quality, namely, that the prominence of quality issues reflects a certain groundswell of disenchantment with, and a public questioning of, the present condition of education. This standpoint emphasizes that although there are no absolute upper boundaries to qualitative success, there are lower limits below which dissatisfaction can slump into a crisis of confidence. This is a useful way of viewing quality insofar as it identifies the linchpin to be the subjective factors of *perceptions* of performance and societal *expectations*, which are themselves changing. They are not necessarily based on objective evidence. As discussed in Chapter 1, schools are now confronted with an inflated and bewildering array of expectations which explains, perhaps as much as any other factor, the current preoccupation with quality. The outstanding question might then be not so much "How can schools do better?" but "What are the implications of expecting so much of them?".

The difficulties that the starting point of dissatisfaction poses as the basis for policy change, however, as opposed to the academic analysis of the quality issue, are considerable. It is unlikely on its own to be an adequate foundation on which constructively to build educational improvement if that means over-reliance on the "stick" of chastisement at the expense of the "carrots" of encouragement and support. It risks alienating the very group crucial to a well-functioning education system — a highly-motivated, professional body of teachers. It risks, too, placing undue weight on vociferous short-term political pressures that will often have immediate electoral advantage as their purpose rather than the welfare of future generations of students. All criticisms cannot be blindly accepted as being equally valid and well-founded especially as they are often made on the flimsiest direct knowledge of what actually takes place in schools. But the emphasis on levels of confidence and the search for legitimacy is illuminating, since it makes the important link between the putatively *objective* enquiry into how well schools and school systems are performing and the manifold *subjective* expectations and public pressures to which they are now exposed.

From the foregoing, we can identify a further aspect of contrasting approaches to the quality issue. There are those who claim that schools and school systems in general are in "crisis" in comparison with others who, while identifying problem areas, believe the system to be functioning relatively well and that will bring about the desired improvements through incremental changes. Simply as an illustration, it is instructive to compare the tenor of the introductory sentences of well-publicised national reports released in two of the OECD countries most associated with official concern for school quality — the United States and the United Kingdom. "Our Nation is at risk" is the apocalyptic warning that begins one[3], while "there is much to admire in our schools" are the words that begin the description of the present situation in the widely distributed summary of the United Kingdom official report *Better Schools*[4]. It needs to be added that the notion of "crisis", as well as becoming rapidly devalued through over-use, encompasses very differing perceptions of what there is seen to be a crisis of — whether of confidence, of performance, of provision, of professional motivation, of goals and expectations, of knowledge, or some combination of these.

The third main reason why not everyone can agree with system-wide goals being invoked as the basis for the delineation and assessment of quality is that, for many, the quality of schooling has crucially to do with the teaching/learning process and what students actually learn; it is only secondarily related to such general aims as, for example, realising equality of opportunity or the liberal exercise of parental or student choice. Yet, using the latter aims of educational policy as examples of the criteria by which to assess the achievement of quality — that is, goals that apply system-wide — would require that that assessment have a negative result so long as equality is not realised or the exercise of choice remains limited, where these are accepted goals. The approach will differ markedly, therefore, according to whether all educational goals inform perceptions and assessments of the quality of school systems or only a certain set of goals that are perceived to be directly pertinent to student learning. In other words, the question arises: "quality of what?"

c) **Quality of what?**

Delineating which aims should be given priority thus raises the central issue of which aspects of educational performance should enter the overall specification of quality. Related to much of the discussion are the distinctions between inputs, processes, and outcomes. For many people, "quality" is predominantly about outcomes. Implicit here is a mixture of applied common-sense and metaphors borrowed from economics. Whether a new car or house is of high quality is not judged ultimately by the rational owner in terms of the materials that went into their manufacture or the time it took to construct them but whether or not they function satisfactorily. Similarly, so the common-sense argument runs, whether schools and school systems are of high quality should be judged ultimately by the standard of their "products". To pursue the example, this would imply focusing on the achievements of the students that emerge from schools rather than on the resources — financial, physical, or human — expended in the process. Such a line of reasoning may be seen as a reaction to the previous period of rapid quantitative expansion experienced in many countries, implying a shift in emphasis from quantity to quality though as stated previously in this chapter and in Chapter 8, the relation between quality and quantity is interactive, and many current proposals for reform would entail significant new expenditures. On this view, the focus on outcomes is seen as a corrective to an over-emphasis on inputs.

The common-sense argument for paying closer attention to outcomes is certainly a powerful one. But the comparisons with acquiring a new car or house are misleadingly simplistic, as much because of the problematic nature of the very distinctions of inputs/processes/outcomes, as because of the risk of misunderstanding the actual relations between them.

First, even assuming that input/output terminology can be meaningfully applied to the educational field, it would be mistaken to argue that a revived focus on outcomes implies that inputs and process become accordingly less important. On the contrary, once assessments of quality lead to suggestions of how improvements can be implemented, then factors such as teaching skills and approaches, appropriate curricula, adequate facilities and textbooks, and the very organisation of schools, all come to the fore. In other words, it is misleading, if not wrong, to interpret attention to educational outcomes as implying the relative downgrading of the determinants that lead to them. Indeed, an approach to improving quality that does not focus on the links between these different factors in a holistic way is destined to fail.

Equally fundamental is the fact that, so far as the recent preoccupation with qualitative factors has stemmed from a growing awareness of the active, two-way nature of the teaching/learning process and the complex chemistry of schools often called "ethos", then it has actually served to undermine the applicability of mechanistic input/output terminology and models of schooling. In other words, intertwined in the advocacy of greater concern for quality are two potentially contradictory strands of thinking: on the one hand, that the emphasis should shift from inputs to outputs; on the other, that the input/output distinction is a distortion that neglects the complex set of processes involved in determining outcomes.

These warnings against the neglect of the determinants of outcomes through over-emphasis on those outcomes alone do not negate the validity of, indeed necessity for, being concerned about what schools actually do and what children actually learn. The defining purposes of schools are, as always, teaching and learning and it would be dubious casuistry if awareness of the complexities involved was used to argue that these purposes no longer matter. Whether from the standpoint of the classroom teacher or from that of education authorities, how and what children learn lies at the heart of the process of schooling.

Given this, it should still be fully recognised that the term "outcomes" is open to a broad range of possible meanings. Further dimensions need still to be elaborated in delineating different possible approaches to quality in schooling. *Should priority in definitions of "quality" be given to those outcomes specifically defined as cognitive (or still more narrowly drawn if qualified as "basic") or should they embrace a broader understanding of the purposes of education to include affective, social, aesthetic, and moral learning.* This question will be discussed in subsequent chapters. Here, it needs to be underlined that the concern for quality should not be assumed to comprehend primarily the evidence of cognitive test scores. Indeed, on close scrutiny it emerges that many of those who allege that standards have declined and who clamour for a return to basics are precisely those who are equally incensed about supposedly deteriorating moral values, inadequate preparation for citizenship, and insufficient regard for such social graces as neatness, punctuality, and politeness. Contrary to the impression left by an extensive literature that regards "quality" as synonymous with "level of cognitive outcomes", if only implicitly through the absence of other sorts of indicators, this identity cannot be assumed even for those who place most faith in measured pupil attainment scores.

The fact remains that priorities and emphases do differ crucially over the degree to which levels of cognitive achievement among pupils and students are treated as the paramount indicators of quality.

A closely related point is that the traditions and cultures of OECD countries span a wide spectrum of conviction regarding the priority to be attached to measuring outcomes as a precondition of improving them. In part, this corresponds to the contrast between emphasis on "quality control", on the one hand, and on establishing the conditions and environment in which high quality is believed to flourish, on the other, even if the two are not mutually exclusive. Issues of assessment and evaluation are taken up repeatedly throughout this report and in Chapters 4 and 7 in particular. Suffice it to say in this context that assessment alone should not be assumed to be a *sufficient* condition for raising the level of outcomes, however valuable a contribution it may make.

A final word on outcomes is appropriate. Children in school are not passive receptacles, there simply to be "filled up". Up to ten years of their lives will be spent in compulsory school, and in all likelihood several more in pre-primary and post-compulsory institutions. The nature of the school experience and its environment cannot be ignored. If a child reaches adolescence, brilliant in test performance but bored or insecure, something has evidently gone amiss. Schooling is preparation for adult life but not exclusively so. It has also become in itself a prolonged period of each person's lifetime. Over-reliance on the economic metaphors of "outputs" and "products" may have the unintended effect of diminishing the value of schooling as a life-enhancing experience of itself.

d) Quality for whom?

There are considerable differences of focus along the dimension of the achievement levels of pupils -- for some the quality issue is about nothing if not about the low-achiever, for some, it is predominantly about the gifted and high-achievers, while others insist that the perspective must embrace all pupils in schools. In reality, no country formally denies that the responsibility of its education services is to ensure the best possible schooling for all pupils. The OECD Ministers of Education declared when they met in Paris in 1984 that:

"The goal of educating each child to the limits of her or his ability remains paramount in view of the need to build the future of democratic and increasingly pluralistic societies on the many different talents of young people...".[5]

But they also added, "with special efforts for the disadvantaged and the handicapped". That emphasis is important. For much of the present attention paid to quality, and the criticisms levelled at current levels of school performance derive from the perception that the achievement levels of too many young people are unacceptably low because they are receiving either too little education or education of the wrong sort, or both. The major priority is thus to enhance the amount of appropriate learning and schooling that they receive.

The low-achiever is not the sole target group. Some elitists look to the other end of the scholastic ladder and complain that academically gifted pupils are being swamped by mediocrity. For them, quality means having a proper respect for excellence. Others, with no ideological axe to grind, are no less anxious to stretch the eager minds of higher achievers. Those who rate education's most important role as maintaining their country's economic competitiveness, and who believe that this should be predominantly accomplished through the production of highly-skilled scientists and technologists, have an interest in developing bright children with particular aptitudes in such subjects as mathematics.

Where the emphasis is placed along the continuum of low and high achievement is in part influenced by ideology — "excellence" being a hallowed rallying cry for the traditionalist just as "equality" and concern for the disadvantaged are the flags of the progressive and egalitarian — though it is quite consistent for either to be concerned about the attainment levels of pupils at both ends of the spectrum of scholastic success. In fact, there is a danger that, in their search for a clear focus and the identification of priorities, policy-makers may neglect the large middle group of pupils whose abilities are at the average. The challenge for school policies is how to raise the attainment levels of all pupils.

A related but distinct dimension concerns the degree to which the focus is on the school population as a whole or on special groups or sections of the school population each with special claims. The dimension outlined in the previous paragraphs concerns priorities in terms of groups of the school population defined by ability and attainment using *standard norms of achievement.* Increasingly, particular interest groups or sections of the population are questioning the validity of these norms. For them, schooling should also have the capacity of adapting to satisfy their interests rather than seeking to bring these particular students in line with dominant or conventional standards. These claims are raised most sharply today by, or on behalf of, girls, cultural minorities, and the handicapped. From an equality perspective, the distinction is between the application of universal standards that define pupils as high, medium, or low achievers (which then focuses attention on the disadvantage of those who are repeatedly found to be among the least successful) and the emergence of *special claims* and the challenge this poses to universal standards. Instead of disadvantage compared with the rest, the latter perspective is of *rights based on special identity*.

The perceived shortcomings that emerge from viewing developments through these two perspectives may overlap: the disabled may well claim that they have traditionally been educationally disadvantaged and that this disadvantage will be ameliorated through mainstream schooling whatever the other arguments for integration[6]; children belonging to certain cultural minorities are disproportionately found among low-achievers and school drop-outs and may see a solution in programmes that fully recognise their cultural heritage[7]; girls, most especially from lower socio-economic status groups, have traditionally fared badly and may blame the fact that schools and curricula remain male-dominated[8]. But despite the overlap, these two approaches are not necessarily the same and the argument for special consideration based on identity applies whether or not there is demonstrable evidence of educational disadvantage.

The distinction is of particular relevance to the quality debate. Even when overall levels of educational attainment are adjudged to be generally satisfactory, certain sections of the population will dispute the criteria used for the assessment unless their needs and claims have been fully taken into account. To take one example only, the advocates of integrating the handicapped into schools can question whether a high-quality schooling is available unless there is widespread opportunities for the disabled to participate in ordinary classrooms *whether or not that integration results in higher average attainment levels.* How far recognition of special claims can go, or else how far conventional norms can change to accommodate them, are questions of far-reaching significance for the exercise of defining general standards and the construction of indicators of quality — the topics of the next chapter.

Answers to the question "quality for whom?" can thus begin to define a radical conception of equality of opportunity that goes beyond the distribution of attainment to encompass the locus of participation and control in present-day education systems. As expressed by one analyst of equality in education[9]:

"For all groups in society, access to influence and control over education, its content and methods, is as important a dimension of equality with other groups as any quantitive measure of educational attainment. If equal participation in education by different groups will have any meaning as a measure of equality in educational terms, a precondition must be that the groups also have an equal share in deciding what education shall be about."

While "quality" and "equality" are not identical concepts — in the abstract, the former ultimately refers to levels and standards while the latter at root focuses on the distribution of benefits and power — at the practical level, they are extremely hard to disentangle. This is because they are so inter-related even conceptually, because they are based on educational values and ideologies that cut across both concepts, and because it is extremely difficult in practice to decompose any given policy or decision into its "quality" aspects, on the one hand, and its "equality" components, on the other. There is no single relationship between them but many, depending on the political values adopted and the aspects of education in question. Those who assert a clear contrast between excellence and equality, or who deny any tension at all between these concepts ignore this complexity.

CONCLUDING REMARKS

It would be repetitive to conclude by underlining the complexity of quality in basic education. In fact, this chapter has attempted to move towards a measure of clarification by delineating some of the major assumptions and dimensions that lie behind it. This exercise has value in its own right. But it has a double purpose that extends beyond clarification for its own sake. First, it reinforces the starting point of this report, which was to recognise the variety of interpretations of quality rather than proffer an OECD definition. To have offered a definition would have dictated a partisan stance towards each of the different dimensions of quality that have been identified.

Secondly, educational debate and value positions have become more complex and confusing, not to say confused, over recent years rendering simple contrasts such as left versus right, progressive versus traditionalist, egalitarian versus elitist, increasingly inadequate to describe the lines along which agreements and disagreements can be drawn. The factors behind this are many, including the greater politicisation of schooling and the sharper competition concomitant with the cutbacks in the growth of educational expenditure. No less important is the fact that so many of the ideas for educational change canvassed in recent times have now been tried in some form, evaluated, and found wanting. With the scepticism born of experience that distinguishes the 1980s from the 1960s, grand principles and all-embracing educational theory have lost much of their appeal and it becomes increasingly difficult to discern some key ideas about policies and practice that will command wide support.

The present interest in quality is not simply a reaction to the 1960s and the prominence of the equity goal at that time. The relationships between quality and equality are far too intertwined and subtle to be crudely contrasted. The very nature of educational debate has moved on during this time too. An inherent difficulty in grasping the quality concept is precisely that the informed scepticism, referred to above, has ruled out the possibility of formulating a small number of grand principles that could be taken as the basis of a "new theory of quality". But here is a possible danger. Many politicians and media representatives demand the clear messages and prognoses that grand theory allows. In the face of this demand, the caveats of education administrators and teachers can sound distinctly cautious and evasive. The latter then risk being left aside as others come forward with their own responses to outstanding challenges. Some of these may make an impact. Others will fall foul of the very obstacles the educationists would have warned against. A cycle of dissensus and disillusion could thus set in at the very time when a new consensus is required. Society-wide reappraisals of aims and missions, as proposed in the conclusion of the previous chapter, cannot succeed if undertaken in an atmosphere of suspicion and intolerance.

NOTES AND REFERENCES

1. Australian Government Publishing Service (1985), *Quality of Education in Australia: Report of the Review Committee* (Chairman: Peter Karmel), Canberra. p. 3.
2. Lundgren, U. (1987), *New Challenges for Teachers and their Education*, Standing Conference of European Ministers of Education Background Report, Council of Europe, Strasbourg.
3. National Commission on Excellence in Education (1983), *A Nation at Risk: The Imperative for Education Reform*, U.S. Department of Education, Washington, D.C.
4. Department of Education and Science, London and Welsh Office (1985), *Better Schools: A Summary*, HMSO, London.
5. OECD (1985), "OECD Ministers Discuss Education in Modern Society", Paris (document on general distribution), p. 45.
6. See OECD/CERI (1981), *The Education of the Handicapped -- Integration in the School*, Paris; and OECD/CERI (1985), *Integration of the Handicapped in Secondary Schools*, Paris.
7. See OECD/CERI (1987), *Immigrants' Children at School*, Paris; and OECD/CERI (1987), *Multicultural Education*, Paris.
8. See OECD (1986), *Girls and Women in Education*, Paris.
9. Eide, K. (1978), "Some Key Problems of Equality in Education", Paper prepared for IIEP/Inter-Agency Seminar on "Inequalities in Educational Development", 27-30 November.

Chapter 3

THE CONTROVERSIAL ISSUE OF STANDARDS

INTRODUCTION

"Are standards falling?" has become the most controversial question in education today. Educational researchers often find themselves under criticism for having failed to provide unequivocal answers to the question based on empirical evidence. But then such answers as are presented — whether by politicians, the media, or in educational debate more widely — often appear to manipulate evidence in order to validate preconceived positions. In part, this derives from the "politicisation" of education described already. It follows too from the variety of meanings and interpretations of the term "standards" and from the inherent difficulties of broaching the seemingly simple question that begins this paragraph. These matters are discussed in this chapter.

It is necessary, to begin with, to make the position of this chapter clear on one central matter. A concern about the cognitive outcomes of schooling is not inimical to the ideal of equality of opportunity. On the contrary, only by being concerned about low levels of cognitive achievement can societies hope to raise them to satisfactory levels. It is pointless to bemoan the fact that too many leave school with too little to show for it unless serving the learning needs of this group becomes a central priority of education policies. Equally, it ill serves the disadvantaged to avoid confronting their learning difficulties and to offer "soft" options instead.

THE MEANING OF STANDARDS

Etymologically, a standard is: the degree of excellence required for particular purposes; an accepted or approved example against which others are judged or measured; or (often plural), a principle of integrity, propriety, or honesty. What is most striking about these definitions is that none corresponds particularly closely with the common educational usage that is, first, expressed in the *plural* form "standards" and, second, refers to *actual* measured levels of educational attainment. The dictionary instead defines a standard as a model, measure, or yardstick against which performance is to be judged and not the results of performance once measurements have been carried out.

Standards as societal expectations

This has led some to suggest that, strictly speaking, standards can neither rise nor fall since they are the fixed barometers of performance and, in this sense, absolute[1]. This interpretation might be questioned in that the criteria or yardsticks of what is expected of education can change and, indeed, have changed perceptibly in recent times. In other words, with the rising yet increasingly manifold expectations of education, standards have gone up though they have also become more confused. Thus, far from "standards" and "average attainment levels" being synonymous, dissatisfaction arises from an apparent dissonance between them. Here the conclusion reached above can be re-emphasized: there is considerable benefit to be gained from continually revising a society-wide definition of standards in the light of new social and economic conditions and in the light of the change, perhaps radical, that is feasible, given the existing institutional frameworks and constraints of school systems.

This, then, is the most general and, arguably, most accurate sense of the term; "standards" are not absolute or fixed but critically reflect societal expectations. Yet therein lies, at the same time, the difficulty of applying such an interpretation in practice. For, different sections of the community have different expectations. Even the same individual may hold varying expectations — for example parents may well apply different criteria depending on whether they are assessing how well the system meets their wishes for their own children (which in a competitive school system will understandably be that their children should receive the "best", even if that is at the expense of others) or whether they are judging the performance of the system as a whole. In the second case, altruistic principles of citizenship can be more generously applied. It is relevant at this point to observe that the current advocacy in some quarters of educational improvement through the untrammelled exercise of parental choice presupposes that the sum total of the "selfish" actions of parents on behalf of their children will in the aggregate result in the most beneficial outcomes for all.

Standards as educational aims

The search for a more precise definition of "standards" can lead in the direction of officially established aims. Decisions about running schools are vested in specific bodies and political institutions which are charged with the task of converting societal expectations into educational aims and strategies. From this follows a second meaning of the term: they are the specific aims of the education system produced through its established decision-making channels which can serve as the yardsticks against which performance should be assessed. On this argument, societal expectations in their generality are not precise enough, let alone sufficiently consistent, to provide clear-cut criteria by which to assess educational performance, and so more specific aims need to be applied as the basis of common and usable standards. Where more obvious a place to look than in the lists provided by the established education authorities?

At first sight, this interpretation satisfies the need for accountability by locating the determination of standards squarely in the political domain. But, in fact, part of the very malaise that caused the concern for quality to surface in the first place is the claim in some quarters that the traditional educational establishment should not be left to determine the aims of schools and schooling and that external opinion — whether that of employers, parents, or particular sectors of the community — must be more closely heeded. In other words, in the name of greater accountability, there is a rejection or qualification of the assumption that society's wishes are best determined by public servants charged with the duty of listening to outside signals, translating those signals into concrete aims, and ensuring that they are realised.

Even if standards accurately reflect each education system's aims, the fact remains that they are not fixed and immutable but over time subject to change through a complex process of political negotiation. It should be added that even in those countries where pressures towards greater external accountability are as yet relatively slight, simple lists of official aims and objectives are of questionable use in determining applicable standards unless they are specific enough to provide criteria by which the performance of the system can be judged, and unless they recognise the trade-offs that frequently must be made between one laudable aim and another. This is a major issue to be confronted in the development of an international set of educational indicators and is discussed in more detail at the end of the chapter.

Standards as average levels of attainment

Concern to enhance external accountability can provide another way of giving precision to the first, "sociological" interpretation of educational standards. This is to reason that many people do in fact expect individual schools to pay closer attention to the measured attainment levels of their pupils, and this implies using standardized tests that allow comparisons across time and across different regions or parts of the education system. Where this is so, the "sociological" definition and the common *de facto* usage that equates standards with actual measured attainment levels come together — the third interpretation of the term "standards".

This usage is also problematic. One obvious difficulty with the application of the notion of accountability in order to equate what society expects with judgements based on the results of measured cognitive tests is that it, too, does not command universal assent, or at least the assertion that this is what people want is meaningless without detailed specification about precisely what is being measured. That in the same quarters where support for some form of national testing is most pronounced there is also an increasingly intensive search for indicators of educational performance that cover a much more inclusive range of the inputs, processes, and outcomes of schooling can itself be taken as *prima facie* evidence that simple averages of student attainment are understood to denote a deficient range of "standards". This results partly from the restriction only to cognitive knowledge and skills. As already noted, even the most convinced advocates of mastery of "basics" are rarely concerned solely with cognitive performance. Most expect much more of schooling than that, all the more so as schools have assumed socialisation responsibilities that previously belonged to families, churches, and communities.

But even within this restriction, it should be recognised that the cognitive domain itself defines anything but a narrow field. Unless the dubious assumption is made that all types of knowledge and abilities are entirely interchangeable and equally useful, there remains a very wide leap from asserting that greater attention should be given to cognitive outcomes and translating this into an acceptable curriculum (see Chapter 4). There is no less a wide difference between mastering the so-called "basics" using memory and rote learning and the acquisition of the creative, higher-order skills that are increasingly being identified as typifying the needs of the modern world that young people enter on leaving school. Arguments that equate national standards with average performance levels can come dangerously near to assuming that all knowledge, skills, and abilities — cognitive and non-cognitive, basic and higher-order — are so closely correlated that *indications of distributions or trends regarding any one is an adequate indication of all.*

A further problem with the "average attainment levels" approach is of a different kind: it makes the definition of standards highly dependent on, and sensitive to, the measuring instruments available at any given point in time. There is the well-known, trenchant factor that certain aspects of learning, school subjects, and types of knowledge and skills are much more amenable to measurement than others. More generally, this approach risks making education policy and practice dependent on, rather than the determinant of, the accepted standards that would emerge when such assessment of performance is a regular feature of the school system. The objection here is not to national assessment *per se* (discussed further in Chapters 4 and 7). It is, rather, with assigning to an instrument or set of instruments a determining role in the definition of national standards. The concern here is twofold. First, if standards are what *should* be, care must be taken not to confuse this with what *is* — values and priorities must still be made clear. Second, national assessment alone will not provide an accurate and comprehensive picture of what is. As two prominent commentators on national assessment programmes conclude:

> "At best, the results of national assessment provide one piece of a puzzle, the broader meaning of which will become clear only if it can be joined with other pieces of information about what is happening in the society and its schools, individually and collectively, across the nation."[2]

The notion of standards

None of the above approaches to standards, therefore, provides unproblematic guides to policy. The more precision that is given to specifying "standards", the more they may be open to the criticism of partiality; the blunter the precision, the less do they provide usable criteria that can be endorsed, rejected, or improved. This does not mean that the notion of "standards" falls to the ground. It is instead a reminder that the search for technical exactitude is not a substitute for the inexact and complex negotiation of educational aims and values. That the common form of the word "standards" is plural is already a warning of this. It leaves unstated and unspecified what their contents are. It refers to a *cluster*, not a single criterion or "standard", leaving open exactly how membership of that cluster of measures is to be decided. The notion of standards, despite the common semblance of a basis in hard, incontrovertible fact, is rarely far removed from a social and political theory of education.

METHODOLOGICAL PROBLEMS AND POLITICAL CHOICES

The proper role of research and use of evidence in the areas discussed above raise some of the most difficult questions to be addressed in an impartial analysis of quality. It has been repeatedly emphasized how subjective and political is the concept and hence the degree to which evidence is thereby shaped and its application predetermined. But that cannot, as a consequence, leave the field to purely ideological debate and the dismissal of scientific enquiry. Despite the degree to which policy questions and the treatment of key issues are subjectively influenced, answers to specific questions still depend on arbitrating matters of fact. Research can play the invaluable role of qualifying or contradicting flawed assertions about educational practice. It is to be hoped that the clarification of aims and values will also clarify the scope for empirical verification. But there is reason for disquiet that the immediate claims of political accountability may ride roughshod over the more cautious assertions of research to such a degree that caveats and riders will be overlooked. The search for simple answers to such a complex question as "are standards falling?", has arguably much more to do with accountability than with scientific enquiry, yet there is no value in those answers, whether politically inspired or not, unless they can be validated[3].

Rising or falling standards?

A telling illustration of the politically-charged drift of the seemingly simple question "are standards falling?" is that the opposite question is rarely asked. Throughout this century, there has been recurring criticism that achievement levels have compared badly with those of the past. Given that most national school systems were in their infancy at the turn of the century, it strains credibility to suppose that the entire period has been one of uninterrupted decline. Allegation of falling standards are probably as much the product of short memories as of genuine educational decline. In any event, current societal expectations of what all youngsters should learn is much higher than in past decades.

Many assertions about standards pay scant attention to what they are or what they should be. Blanket criticisms are commonplace. The difficulties inherent in seeking intelligible answers to the question of improvement or decline thus need to be more sharply defined. They touch on both methodological issues and those of political values.

First, it is essential to recognise the *complexity* of the facts themselves. Taking only student test-score trends in one country (in this case, the United States which has a considerably larger data base than any of the other OECD countries), Marshall Smith, in a review prepared for the OECD, is at pains to emphasize that the trends are neither simple nor unidirectional:

> "*Declining test scores*. This is the most widely touted of the trends and generally considered as a uniformly negative indicator. In fact, the situation is more complex than most observers have the patience to consider. The facts seem to be:
>
> a) Over the decade after 1955 most test scores increased, peaking between 1963 and 1965. Scores on both the Scholastic Aptitude Tests (SATs) and standardized achievement tests followed this pattern.
>
> b) During the period from 1965 to 1972-75 there was a general decline in scores. Two-thirds of the approximately 0.25 standard deviation decline in SAT scores during this period was associated with a changing population, as more minorities had the opportunity to take the college entrance examinations. Other statewide and nationally administered standardized tests also showed a clear drop in scores. The National Assessment of Educational Progress (NAEP) started in the late sixties and early seventies; reading, science, and mathematics scores showed a slight decline on the NAEP from the late 1960s to the mid-1970s for 9, 13, and 17 year-olds. Also during this period, results from international comparisons showed that US students were scoring in the low middle of technologically advanced nations.
>
> c) From 1972-75 to 1982 there was a further decline of approximately 0.2 of a standard deviation in SAT scores, this time apparently not directly associated with a change in

population. A slightly smaller decline showed up for a sample of the total twelfth-grade population in comparisons of the National Longitudinal Survey and the High School and Beyond samples. And in the NAEP, seventeen year-olds showed very slight declines in reading and mathematics. At the other ages there were positive results on the NAEP. Nine and thirteen year-olds showed small but consistent gains in reading and in mathematics. But Blacks (and in reading, Hispanics), especially those in poor families or in the South, showed substantial gains at ages 9 and 13. (This increase may have been caused by changes in schooling resulting from the desegregation of Southern schools in 1969-1972). Also on the positive side, the number of high school students who took advanced placement examinations increased in mathematics and science, while the advanced test score averages remained the same or increased. Thus, there is some indication that both the bottom and the top of the distribution were improving slightly while the middle may have drifted downward.

d) Since 1982 there has been a slight increase in SAT scores and in NAEP scores for 9 and 13 year-olds. The SAT increases may be due to changes in the population. NAEP reading scores for 17 year-olds declined during this period. Recent international comparisons have indicated that the US does a mediocre job.

e) Perhaps of greatest significance, overall since 1968 as shown by NAEP mathematics scores, there has been a slight general decline in average ability to solve complex problems."[4]

Smith certainly does not deny that there are grounds for concern and he emphasizes that other components of educational change, in addition to the evidence of individual test scores, should be taken into account in any discussion of standards and quality. The essential requirement is to recognise the complexity of what the available evidence shows, both within and across countries.

Second, there are formidable technical and educational difficulties in assessing *change*. Fixing bench-marks against which progress or decline is to be assessed is notoriously difficult. Findings are also extraordinarily sensitive to the instruments and measures used. For example, the Karmel report in Australia compared the results of tests administered in 1975 and 1980 and found that "on all other tasks tested there was no significant difference in performance between 1975 and 1980 ... in no case at either age level did performance decline" but noted, for example, among the specific findings singled out for comment that "when reading a newspaper, 26 per cent more of the 10 year-olds (about 68 000 students) and 11 per cent more of the 14 year-olds (about 26 000) were successful in 1980"[5]. It is not plausible to suppose that Australian primary education was 25 per cent more effective at teaching reading at the end of the 1970s than at the mid-point of the decade. But then if such indicators of rising standards are unreliable, doubts must be expressed when the graphs show a downturn. Many of the relatively small changes seized upon as indicators of rising or falling standards are not a sufficient basis from which to deduce significant trends.

How measures are treated often depends on the story they are seen to tell. A good example here is the use of the results of public examinations in the United Kingdom debate. Those who insist that standards have risen over the years point to rising participation rates in examinations as the best available corroborating evidence. The same notes are consistently dismissed by disbelievers as a downwardly moving bench-mark because of their reliance on norm-referencing. Yet, many of the same disbelievers use precisely this indicator in an attempt to show the failings of secondary schools, and support the idea of publishing each school's examination results as the best guide to parents of how one school compares with another. It is at this point, *vice versa*, that the original advocates of improvement are likely to emphasize the unreliability of examinations.

More far-reaching still than the technical hazards of measuring change are those that reside in the very nature of education itself. As presented by one prominent analyst (here in relation to latent trait theories):

> "... these technical criticisms pale into insignificance beside the educational criticisms. The essence of the process of education is to achieve change in behaviour, change that is (in practice if not in theory) not identical in each individual. The invariance of item parameters (apart from a scaling constant) implied by the Rasch model sits unhappily with the notion of educational change."[6]

Third, questions arise concerning the use of *averages* as the "standards" that should be compared over time. In a review of different measures of educational standards and quality, John Keeves points out that while average achievement levels may fall as more students stay on to a further level in the schooling cycle, schools are nonetheless more productive, if only by dint of helping those additional students to attain that level, and this should enter any overall assessment through the calculation of a "yield measure of achievement":

> "The mean level of achievement of a group of students from a system is influenced adversely by the holding power, assessed by the retention rate, operating within the system. However, the system that has succeeded in holding a higher proportion of the age group at school has increased effectively the productivity of the system, even if there were a decline in the average level of achievement of the students. This led Postlethwaite and his colleagues to develop a composite index [which] provides an assessment of 'how many of the students in the system are brought how far' and is referred to as the productivity of a system or 'yield'."[7]

Keeves notes that brave methodological assumptions must be made *en route* to such estimates. The educational problems of interpretation are no less daunting. Critics convinced that "more means worse" will not have their fears allayed by reference to increasing retention rates as a good in itself unless tangible benefits are also seen to result from staying longer in school and college. Retention alone, in other words, is a dubious measure of productivity, though a reasonable comparison may well be between the demonstrable benefits of young people remaining in education set against what otherwise would have happened had they left school earlier. Once again, the search for clear messages from simple indicators comes up against the complexity of educational and social change.

Whether or not retention rates are a direct indicator of a school system's "productivity", a more general point emerges from the fact that the student body in schools has altered markedly over recent decades. Changes in average test scores over time have been shown, as Smith reports above, to depend significantly on the evolution of the composition of that body. This has led some to look for "adjusted measures of achievement" to take account of the different social and ethnic origins of students. The point is a simple and powerful one: if valid comparisons are to be made, whether over time or across parts of a system or country, "like should be compared with like" and account taken of the different social intake into schools. Measures of quality should reflect, that is, the inequalities in students' social backgrounds.

Presumably, schools should not be held accountable for social and environmental factors beyond their control. Relevant in assessing the performance of schools is what they have contributed to learning over and above the raw material represented by the pupil intake. If the focus is upon individual schools, as opposed to an average "value-added" estimate over the system as a whole, then it will often be the case that institutions with generally lower achievement levels will have been more effective at enhancing student learning — have added more — than schools with higher scores (though how far parents, in choosing which establishment to send their offspring, would be impressed sufficiently by such evidence to select a "higher value-added/lower average score" school is an open question).

The point about making such adjustments is a simple one but how they should be made and interpreted are, however, less straightforward. It is one thing to make a single adjustment using a coefficient for the effect of social background — even then it is likely to be a proxy measure that does not capture the full variety of the effect of differing backgrounds. It is quite another to propose that what is then "left over" is the sole responsibility of schools. In other words, accurate estimation of the "value-added" by a school or schools involves a complicated calculation that should take account of *all* environmental factors beyond the control of schools, not just the nearest social proxy coefficient to hand. The adjustment is rendered still more complex by the finding derived from the International Association for the Evaluation of Educational Achievement (IEA) data that the ratio of home to school factors in explaining the learning of different school subjects varies markedly. Home and social variables account for a major portion of variance explained in reading, for example; the balance is reversed for learning a foreign language. In the latter case, the cultural capital of social background plays a less decisive role than the curricular and pedagogic accomplishments of the teacher and the school[8]. A note on "adjusted measures of achievement" is warranted. For the purposes of making valid comparisons between schools or school districts, such adjustments are necessary, but for demonstrating how far behind the high-flyers are the low-achievers, such adjustments may be misleading. A major reason for the current concern about the quality of schooling is precisely that certain groups of pupils and students consistently perform below the level of others, thereby underlining again just how closely the issues of quality and equality interact. Systematically to remove evidence of this through statistical control runs the risk of obliterating a major argument for change.

Considerations of both equality and quality suggest, therefore, that a further refinement of the comparison of averages is the comparison of the *distribution* of results. Postlethwaite[9], for example, has shown in a re-examination of the data recorded in the 1970 IEA Science Study that, if the mean achievement of the bottom 50 per cent of the 14 year-olds is examined between countries, striking differences emerge that are not readily apparent when only a comparison of the overall mean scores and measures of variability is conducted. The score of the 25th percentile (of this bottom half of students) in England, for example, is below the median (50 percentile) scores of this group in Germany and Japan. A closer look at the Japanese score in mathematics in 1981 shows that it is a system where, comparatively, the average is high, the range of performance of the top half of students is narrow, while the spread of the bottom quarter of students is wide. In other words, where overall averages are the same, wide variations in the performance of the high- and low-achieving groups may well be hidden.

Concerning the gifted at the top of the ability range, certain IEA studies have made comparisons between countries, assessing, for example, the achievement in science of the top one per cent, five per cent, or ten per cent. It has been argued that it would be inappropriate to compare the performances of equal proportions of the students in a given year group on the grounds that in a highly selective system, the level of performance of, say, the top five per cent represents that of a small, very select band in programmes geared to their needs whereas where there are substantial retention rates, the same proportion would represent a less exclusive body of students. Others might reply that this is precisely the reason for such a comparison, namely, to gauge the effects on the élite of different structures of organisation of the school system. In fact, despite differing emphases between systems, no clear relation has been found between the degree of selectivity operating in the school system and the performance levels of a given proportion of gifted pupils[10].

Fourth, the need for caution in the attempt to discern trends in standards derives from the difficulty of establishing the *causes* of the changes observed, even assuming that the facts seem relatively clear. The difficulty of isolating causes is especially acute during periods of rapid social and economic evolution. How far observed change can be attributed to factors within the ambit of responsibility of schools and educational policy is clearly one question that would need to be addressed. Another is how effective the different suggestions for *current* reform would be, even assuming that the causes of *past* trends have been convincingly identified. As concluded in Chapter 1, it is vain to propose recipes based on a return to "the good old days", given that it is doubtful that those days were as good as memory believes or that school policies and practices simply borrowed from the past would have the same effect today.

One source of the difficulty in discerning the causes of change derives from the passage of time itself. Educational benefits from investments tend to be realised over the long term. As a rule, the impact of policies can be appreciated in full, positively or negatively, only when sufficient evidence has been accumulated and this may take many years. Equally, contemporary trends must be placed in their historical context. The necessity of carefully disentangling trends, timing, and possible causes was fully appreciated by the recent United States Congressional Budget Office report on educational achievement in the following terms:

> "Perhaps because of the extensive attention paid to high school tests, many analysts who expect the achievement trends to have educational causes look to the late 1960s and 1970s — when the test scores of senior-high students were falling — for policies that might have caused the decline in scores. Similarly, many expect that the causes of the subsequent upturn can be found in the policies of the 1980s and perhaps the late 1970s. While there is some truth in this view, it too is simpler than the data warrant. Some of the educational changes that contributed to the achievement trends were probably consistent in timing with trends in scores in the lower grades, not with scores at the senior-high level. The cohorts that produced the upturn in test scores entered school beginning in the late 1960s, and their improved performance was evident during their elementary school years. Thus, educational practices as early as the late 1960s and early 1970s — at least in elementary schools — might also have contributed to the rise in scores."[11]

It is a matter of interpretation. There is little to be said for conducting expensive and sophisticated surveys aimed at accurately charting student achievement if the policy conclusions drawn from the findings are hastily conceived and ill-founded.

Standards as expectations

Since one meaning of "standards" is the expectations held by different groups towards schools and schooling, then the search for evidence about those expectations is also part of the exercise of fixing standards. With what degree of satisfaction is educational provision received by the different clienteles, in particular by pupils, parents, and teachers? Do they value the current provision? Could schools better serve the interests of their clienteles? This kind of evidence, through its very subjectivity, should not be considered in isolation from the objective factors and realities that shape these viewpoints. But neither should they be ignored.

The clientele whose views have been little discussed so far in this report are young people themselves. An extensive survey of the views of the young conducted by CERI gives some grounds for comfort insofar as few seem to reject education out of hand:

> "Virtually no country survey of young people's attitudes reveals a rejection of education. Most young people want to learn; they value education and believe that it will better their lives. In many cases, their expectations of what schools ought to do are pitched pretty high."[12]

But perhaps for the very reason that their expectations are high, young people are often dissatisfied with what is actually on offer and are less cautious than many educationists about the wisdom of the school adopting a curriculum that is explicitly vocational and adapted to "useful" life skills. (Although the CERI survey was based largely on evidence gathered before high levels of youth unemployment had become established as a quasi-permanent feature of many OECD countries, but also before a broad range of counter-measures had had effect, it is difficult to speculate on how those views might have changed in the interim). The report continues:

> "Young people are especially critical of the relationship between school and work. They believe that schools are divorced from 'life' and 'life's occupations' and that they are mostly concerned with the next level of education ... The concern that schooling should prepare for occupational roles is widespread among young people. In the 1977 Italian survey, this was the function of schooling that received the most support. Ninety per cent of the upper secondary school pupils recently surveyed in Sweden believe that more practical periods are needed in their curriculum. Thirty-nine per cent of them add that they would rather have a job than go on to upper secondary level; 25 per cent are ready to leave school if offered a job. Substantially similar evidence comes from Australia."[13]

That significant numbers of youngsters express dissatisfaction with their schooling is by no means sufficient evidence with which to condemn schools for a dereliction of duty. They are only partly responsible for those complaints and some dissatisfaction would be expressed in the disgruntlement of adolescence whatever the educational arrangements in place. What is more serious is that the young are joined by parents, teachers, and employers in the general indictment that education succeeds badly in realising the non-cognitive goals they all agree to be among the most important. Findings from several countries point towards similar conclusions:

> "Research by Raven working in the United Kingdom and Ireland, by De Landsheere in Belgium and Johnston and Bachman in the United States shows that, although there are considerable differences in their priorities, most teachers, pupils, ex-pupils, parents and employers think that the main goals of education include fostering self-confidence, the ability to take initiative in introducing change, the ability to work with others, the ability to make one's own observation and learn without instruction and the willingness to work for the good of the community in which one lives. All these authors also show that most teachers and pupils are agreed that these goals are sadly neglected at the present time and, as a result, poorly attained. These opinions are confirmed in studies of the qualities needed at work and in society, and evidence of their neglect is provided by Flanagan."[14]

Such findings raise fascinating and politically charged questions. Are those in political and administrative authority correct when they claim to reflect society's wishes by giving greater priority to cognitive results? What role should opinion and attitudinal polls play in the formulation of objectives and priorities?

Further reflection on reported attitudes might suggest, however, that such findings are as much evidence of inconsistent demands made on schools as of clear indications either of coherent goals or of satisfaction/dissatisfaction levels among education's different clienteles. How far can schools be expected to succeed in developing sufficiently both the non-cognitive traits of initiative, self-confidence, selflessness, and adaptability to change, on the one hand, and in paying greater attention to cognitive achievement, on the other, when both are called for? Nor is it clear — and here considerations of equality re-emerge — that either students or parents would choose the more individualised programmes that might best foster greater independence, initiative, and self-confidence if that in turn would jeopardise the student's chances of competing equally with others for the credentials sought after in the job market. For, despite expressed enthusiasm for the goals of enhancing personal growth and development, the key goal for many parents remains that of their children acquiring the credentials required in today's competition for employment[15]. Whether or not parents apply a different set of attitudes when assessing schools in general and the schooling of their own children — a possibility suggested above — would need to be further clarified before such findings could be interpreted as showing that, at root, they wish for whatever will give their offspring a competitive edge over others. What might be more useful than constructing indices of satisfaction and dissatisfaction levels, however, is the clarification of significant differences among education's main actors, differences that would be less sensitive to the formulation of the questions or the style of enquiry than gauging absolute levels of satisfaction[16].

Reported attitudes present, therefore, certain difficulties of interpretation. It is possible that more "objective" indicators like high drop-out rates among students, or the widespread resort among some parents to expensive educational alternatives, or teacher unrest, are a more telling indication of attitudes than subjective reports. How far are the answers cited in such reports significantly influenced by the questions asked? And since it is likely that the concept of "relative deprivation" applies to education as to other social goods, then those who benefit most from education may well be those who express least satisfaction since they want still more, and this would rule out drawing implications of need directly from expressions of unfulfilled expectations. Finally, a general point, that is equally relevant to the wider quality debate, needs underlining: dissatisfaction with education is much easier to identify than satisfaction. Criticisms, whether from parents, politicians, or employers, are vociferous. Praise is usually muted.

There are, therefore, several reasons why evidence in the form of stated attitudes cannot be used exclusively to ascertain how the various actors in the education process value its present quality. On the other hand, a consideration of attitudes is useful to clarify the goals and priorities that people actually hold, as opposed to those they are assumed to hold, and to establish how significant are the different viewpoints of the different clienteles — for example, teachers and parents, pupils and teachers, one group of parents and another. The views of the young are especially important.

CONCLUDING REMARKS: CLARIFYING STANDARDS

This chapter has sought to dispel the common assumption — that educational standards is a term widely understood and that there is general agreement about what constitutes standards. The chapter has also sought to demonstrate that the exercise of discerning trends in standards over time is fraught with methodological problems.

The chapter has warned against assuming that findings about, and indicators of, student achievement in one area can stand as proxies for performance levels across all relevant fields of knowledge, skills, and appreciation. It has sought further to emphasize how valued are the non-cognitive aims of schooling. Success is not to be narrowly judged by the mechanical ability of students to reproduce basic knowledge and few would be satisfied if this were its primary achievement. On the contrary, with rising expectations, schools are expected to stretch all their pupils as far as possible.

To register that the meaning of "standards" is unclear is not to condemn use of the term; it is certainly not to question the central concern for improving teaching and learning. The lack of precision follows directly from the various nuances of meaning that attach to the term itself and the fact that common usage refers in the plural to a cluster of goals and areas of performance. It derives from the latitude of interpretation that is introduced when translating generally-stated goals into practical action. The task of seeking greater clarity in the definition of standards is, in consequence, a continual process that will always attract controversy. A constant climate of competing claims and political disagreements over education, however, is likely to prove counterproductive to the very desire to raise standards. Individual schools and systems in their entirety need a positive sense of common purpose.

All this suggests that the main purpose of clarification should not be to engage in the endless debate concerning whether standards have risen or fallen. Where dissatisfactions exist, the accomplishments of schools can be set more fruitfully against contemporary and future demands rather than against romantic visions of past achievements. Progress towards clarification can be made on at least three fronts:

a) A general society-wide process of reappraisal and clarification of educational aims and values should be undertaken on which standards can be founded. The aim where possible should be to forge consensus and to avoid the widening of existing rifts or the relentless pursuit of sectional interests.

b) Statistical information and indicators should be developed that, as far as possible, allow genuine debate on agreed questions of fact. These indicators should be constructed so as to reflect the goals of schooling and identify key problem areas that act as barriers to meeting those goals. The identification of indicators will prove problematic to the extent that consensus about the purposes of schooling is absent. Positively put, *a)* and *b)* go hand in hand and are mutually reinforcing.

c) Research enquiry can most usefully provide indications of how different educational arrangements, policy options, and reform strategies affect standards. It is important to move beyond the essentially descriptive exercise of delineating and charting standards to a more informed understanding of how they can be improved. A sophisticated picture of the successes and shortcomings of schools will be largely wasted if it provides the basis for hasty and fallacious conclusions about policies.

There has recently emerged widespread international interest in educational indicators. The call for better and more relevant information on the functioning of schools is now audible both from within education systems and from bodies outside their traditional ambit. Two international conferences on indicators and evaluation, jointly sponsored by the OECD and the national authorities in the United States and France respectively, have been recently staged[17] (see Chapter 7).

It is certainly important to extend the knowledge base on which educational decisions are taken. The very process of developing indicators can help to clarify and forge agreement on fundamental goals and values. But they will never reflect the totality of what is understood to be quality in schooling; they can only provide a partial picture as the proponents of indicator development are themselves at pains to point out[18]. Nor do indicators provide technocratic solutions that circumvent the need to address the values and assumptions on which they are based. No matter how well constructed technically, indicators are only as useful as there is acceptance of the assumptions underpinning them. They cannot provide absolute readings of educational "health". There is, in other words, no technical way of skirting around the subjective nature of the quality concept.

NOTES AND REFERENCES

1. See, for example, Wright, N. (1979), "Standards" in Rubenstein, D. (ed.), *Education and Equality*, Penguin, Harmondsworth, pp. 226-239.

2. One interesting source of discussion on the relation between research and policy in the educational field is Husén, T. and Kogan, M. (eds.) (1984), *Educational Research and Policy: How Do They Relate?* Pergamon, Oxford, New York, Toronto, Sydney, Paris, Frankfurt.

3. Power, C. and Wood, R. (1984), "National Assessment: A Review of Programmes in Australia, the United Kingdom, and the United States", *Comparative Education Review*, Vol. 28, No. 3.

4. Smith, M.S. (1986), "Education Reform in the United States" (OECD working document). Report prepared for the joint Italy/OECD Conference on "Quality in Education: The Vital Role of Teachers", held in Rome 6-8 May, 1986. Based on:

   — Educational Testing Service (1986), *The Reading Report Card: Progress Towards Excellence in our Schools. Trends in Reading over Four National Assessments 1971-1989* (report 15-R-01) Princeton, New Jersey.

   — IEA (1985), *United States Summary Report : Second International Mathematics Study*, Stipes Publishing Co., Champaign, Illinois.

   — Koretz, D. (1986), *Trends in Educational Achievement*, Congressional Budget Office, Washington D.C., pp. 36, 38, 44, 154-156.

   — O'Neill, D.M. (1986), *Education in the United States 1940-1983: A Survey of Trends and Current Concerns*, U.S. Bureau of the Census, Center for Demographic Studies, Washington D.C., p. 22.

   — *Phi Delta Kappan* (1985), "SAT Scores Rise for the Fourth Straight Year", Vol. 67, p. 238.

   — Raizen, S.A. and Jones, L.V (eds.) (1985), *Indicators of Precollege Education in Science and Mathematics*, National Academy Press, Washington D.C., pp. 29 and 132.

- Stedman, L. and Kaeslte, C. (1985), "The Test Score Decline is Now Over: Now What?", *Phi Delta Kappan*, Vol. 67, pp. 204-210.
- U.S. National Center for Education Statistics (1983), *Digest of Education Statistics: 1983-1984*, Washington D.C.
- Walker, D.A. (1976), *The IEA Subject Survey: An Empirical Study of Education in Twenty-One Countries*, Almqvist and Wiksell, Stockholm.

5. Australian Government Publishing Service (1985), *Quality of Education in Australia: Report of a Review Committee* (Chairman: Peter Karmel), Canberra.
6. Nuttal, D.L. (1986), "Problems in the Measurement of Change", in Nuttal, D. (ed.), *Assessing Educational Achievement*, The Falmer Press, London.
7. Keeves, J. (1986), "Changing Standards of Performance and the Quality of Education: Concepts and Findings Relevant for Policy-making" (OECD working document). Based on:
   - Postlethwaite, T.N. (1967), *School Organisation and Student Achievement*; Almqvist and Wiksell, Stockholm.
   - Husén, T. (1967), *International Study of Achievement in Mathematics*, Almqvist and Wiksell, Stockholm, and Wiley, New York.
8. Postlethwaite, T.N. (1986), "Research on Quality in Education with Special Emphasis on International Findings" (OECD working document).
9. Postlethwaite, T.N., (1985), "The Bottom Half in Lower Secondary Schooling", in Worswick, G.D.N. (ed.), *Education and Economic Performance*, Gower, London; and Postlethwaite, T.N. (1986), *op. cit.*
10. See, for example, Husén, T. (1983), "Are Standards in U.S. Schools Really Lagging Behind Those In Other Countries?", *Phi Delta Kappan*, Vol. 65, pp. 455-461.
11. The Congress of the United States (1987), *Educational Achievement: Explanations and Implications of Recent Trends*, Congressional Budget Office, Washington D.C., p. xii.
12. OECD/CERI (1983), *Education and Work: The Views of the Young*, Paris, p. 23.
13. OECD/CERI (1983), *ibid.*, p. 24. Based on:
    - Infol-Censis (1977), "Atteggiamenti dei giovani nei confronti del lavoro", *Quaderni di formazione* No. 38-39, Rome, p. 24.
    - A 1978 survey made by a Swedish student organisation (Arbetsmarknaden, 1978:8).
14. Raven, J. (1984), "Some Barriers to Educational Innovation from Outside the School System", *Teachers College Record*, Vol. 85, No. 3, p. 43. Based on:
    - De Landsheere, V. (1984), *La Définition des objectifs pédagogiques*, University of Liège.
    - De Landsheere, V. (1977), "On defining Educational Objectives" in De Landsheere (ed.), *Evaluation in Education*, Vol. 1. Pergamon, London.
    - Flanagan, J.C. and Burns, R.K. (1955), "The Employee Performance Record", *Harvard Business Review*, Vol. 33. pp. 95-102.
    - Flanagan, J.C. (ed.) (1978), *Perspective on Improving Education,* Praeger, New York.
    - Inkeles, A. (1969), "Participant Citizenship in Six Developing Countries", *American Political Science Review*, Vol. 63, pp. 1120-1141.
    - Johnston, L.D. and Bachman, J.G. (1976), "Educational Institutions", in Adams, J.F. (ed.) *Understanding Adolescence* (3rd Edition), Allyn and Bacon, Boston; and McClelland, D.C. and Dailey, C. (1974), *Professional Competencies of Human Science Workers*, McBer and Co., Boston.
    - Raven, J. et al. (1975), *Teachers' Perceptions of Educational Objectives and Examinations*, Irish Association for Curriculum Development, Dublin.

- Raven, J. et al. (1975), *Pupils' Perceptions of Educational Objectives and their Reactions to School and School Subjects*, same publisher.
- Raven, J. (1976), *Pupil Motivation and Values*, same publisher.
- Raven, J. (1977), *Education, Values, and Society*, H.K. Lewis, London; the Psychological Corporation, New York.
- Raven, J. and Dolphin, T. (1978), "The Consequences of Behaving", Report for the Competency Motivation Project, Edinburgh.
- Raven, J. (1981), "The Competences Needed at Work and Society", *CORE*, 5, Vol. 3.
- Raven, J. (1982), "Education and the Competences Needed at Work and in Society", *Higher Education Review*, Vol. 15, pp. 47-57.

15. See findings reported in Raven, J. (1984), *op. cit.*
16. Examples are given in U.S. Center for Education Statistics (1987), *The Condition of Education: A Statistical Report 1987 Edition*, Office of Educational Research and Improvement, Department of Education, Washington D.C., pp. 78-83.
17. Joint United States/OECD International Conference on Educational Indicators held in Washington D.C., 3-6 November, 1987. (See National Center for Education Statistics (1988), *International Conference on Cross-National Education Indicators*, Washington D.C.). Joint France/OECD/CERI Conference on Evaluation of Educational Systems, held in Poitiers, 21-23 March, 1988. See also ministère de l'Education nationale (forthcoming), *Evaluation et indicateurs des systèmes éducatifs*, Paris. For earlier OECD work on educational indicators, see Carr-Hill, R. and Magnussen, O. (1973), *Indicators of Performance of Education Systems*, OECD, Paris.
18. As underlined by, for example, Oakes, J. (1986), *Educational Indicators: A Guide for Policy-Makers*, Center for Policy Research in Education, Occasional Paper, Rutgers University, the Rand Corporation, and the University of Wisconsin-Madison.

Part two

KEY AREAS IN THE PURSUIT OF QUALITY IN SCHOOLS AND SCHOOL SYSTEMS

This part of the report adopts a concrete, policy-oriented approach to quality to complement the conceptual nature of Part One. It discusses a selected number of the key policy areas that are integral components of any broad strategy designed to improve schools and to raise quality throughout systems. The chapters identify major issues and developments in each of these areas, drawing substantially in certain chapters on the discussions and conclusions of the relevant preparatory conferences — on curriculum, on teachers, on evaluation and assessment — that were designed to provide input to this report.

Chapter 4

THE CURRICULUM:
PLANNING, IMPLEMENTATION, AND EVALUATION

CONCEPTS AND DEFINITIONS

The curriculum central to the quality debate

Quality is, then, an elusive concept. When considered in relation to the curriculum, itself chameleon in character, it poses particularly difficult conceptual problems. For how the curriculum is defined, planned, implemented, and evaluated crucially influences the quality of the education that is provided. In this chapter, we shall attempt to define the various ways, implicit or explicit, in which the curriculum is interpreted and applied in practice, and to pinpoint key issues and problems. The ultimate aim is to show how the curriculum might be best designed, implemented, and evaluated so as to ensure a school-based education of quality.

As described in Part One, public attitudes towards the school curriculum have become increasingly critical in recent years. Critics can be divided into two broad categories: *i)* those who chastise schools for departing from traditional or basic subjects and methods and offering a bewildering range of options — that is, for being too progressive; *ii)* those who attack schools for being too slow to make the curriculum relevant to modern society — that is, for being old-fashioned. Each main group can, of course, be sub-divided in several ways. For example, critics condemning the curriculum for being old-fashioned would include those who want schooling to be closer to the contemporary world of work, as well as those who want to see the new curriculum updated while still retaining its traditional liberal character. These differences are necessarily associated with views, often implicit rather than explicit, about what constitutes an education of quality and hence the ways in which the curriculum is defined.

Definitions of curriculum

Definitions of curriculum are fundamental not only because they determine what is taught and learned in schools, but also because they reflect in a subtle form prevailing attitudes towards the purposes of education and the teaching and learning process. Curriculum used to be thought of mainly in terms of subjects and subject matter, of a syllabus or collection of syllabuses. Nowadays it is also perceived as a way of analysing the teaching and learning process in terms that include content as only one of several factors. The new interpretation includes not only what is taught, but how it is taught and why. It thus concerns questions of control, pedagogy, and evaluation.

Skilbeck has suggested that there are three basic educational ideologies, each of which generates a different kind of curriculum and curriculum theory: *a)* Classical Humanism; *b)* Progressivism; *c)* Reconstructionism[1]. All three are, of course, "ideal types", and strands of one or more are to be found in all discussions of what form the curriculum should take:

Classical Humanism is the oldest, originating in Greece in the 4th century B.C., and described in a memorable form by Plato. The ideology continued throughout the Middle Ages and the Renaissance, and was revived in a somewhat different form in the 19th century. It is now sometimes referred to as "elitism" since it suggests that traditional culture is the heritage of only a few rather than the masses. Translated into curriculum theory this educational ideology encourages the view of segregated curricula stratified either according to social position or supposed intellectual capacity. The grammar school curriculum in England, the *lycée* in France, and the *Gymnasium* in Germany and other European countries all share this curriculum theory to some extent, although the continental varieties tend to be more encyclopaedist than the English version, French and German elite curricula having paid more attention to science and technology whereas the English have persisted in a concentration on literary culture. The kind of segregated curriculum that was adopted was critical for the subsequent economic and social development of these societies and economies.

Progressivism goes back at least as far as the 18th century, the ideas of Rousseau[2] being particularly relevant. Whereas Classical Humanism has tended to be "knowledge-centred", Progressivism is "child-centred" and is identified with a romantic rejection of the traditional heritage. Pestalozzi and Froebel continued and developed this tradition in Europe, and Kilpatrick and others developed progressive education in North America in a different way, giving Progressivism a strong social orientation rather than a purely individualistic emphasis.

Reconstructionism might be considered as a development in the 19th and 20th centuries of Progressivism. Dewey, for example, was seeking a modern theory of education appropriate to a democratic and scientific society. In Dewey's writings democracy was seen not simply as a form of government, but as a way of life providing enormous opportunities for experimentation and growth. Reconstructionist education is society-centred, but it is a means of achieving a better life for individuals within that society. The quality of life of individuals is closely connected with the improvement of society itself.

Strands of each of these underlie the different dimensions of the quality concept identified in Chapter 2. It is the reconstructionist ideology that has been dominant in most OECD countries since World War II, although the progressivists and cultural humanists enjoyed a very strong run in the 1960s. Most countries would probably now publicly subscribe to the following list of general principles:

— Education can be a major force for consensual change in society.
— Adherence to a core curriculum, at least during the initial years of schooling, is seen as essential for maintaining social norms and practices.
— At the same time, educational processes should be separated from other social processes, such as political propaganda, commercial advertising, and mass enter-

tainment. Education must, if necessary, enter into conflict with these other processes.
— Education is concerned with producing better and more effective citizens.
— Learning is an active process rather than a passive, teacher-dominated one.
— Teachers are professionally trained agents of cultural transmission and renewal.

It does not follow, of course, that all who subscribe to Reconstructionism would agree on all aspects of curriculum planning; for example, the curriculum can be designed to change society in a variety of ways and even in quite different directions. Translating principles into practice raises key issues that will now be considered.

CORE CURRICULUM

The most important issue concerns the idea of a "core curriculum". Its essential features include the following: it is a *major part* of the whole curriculum; it specifies *content*, usually in such terms as knowledge, skills, and values; it applies to *all schools* in a given system, be it national, regional, or local; it assumes some means of *assessing* outcomes so that the validity of the goals may be verified. It raises conceptual and political issues.

A principle of entitlement is implicit in the relationship between the core curriculum and "quality". If quality in education is understood to mean that all children regardless of sex, ethnic origin, or where they happen to live should be taught essential content and skills up to an acceptable level of achievement, which few would deny, then this establishes a right. This may be expressed in terms of basic skills or of a common cultural heritage or both. Anyone concerned with education is bound to operate with priorities of some kind, differences among which will partly determine which interpretations of quality are adopted, even though the assumptions behind them may often be taken for granted rather than critically examined.

A particular difficulty is that different terminology is often used to convey the idea of core curriculum either in whole or in part. An alternative frequently used is "common curriculum" which overlaps a good deal of the meaning of core curriculum. It is, however, generally used to refer to the whole of the curriculum and curriculum planning rather than the core aspects. "Compulsory curriculum" is also used, often almost as synonymous with the core concept but the term is objectionable for two reasons: first, because the notion of compulsion has undesirable connotations in free societies; secondly, because compulsion is impossible in terms of learning if not in terms of teaching. A more acceptable term is "entitlement curriculum" (see below). This is much more in keeping with notions of education as a right and goes beyond the basic idea of core into expressions of legitimate aspiration.

Thus questions about the curriculum enter into the heart of debates concerning quality. Schools and teachers are often exposed to outside criticism for not getting their priorities right, at least in those systems where greater or less discretion is left to local decision-making. In some countries where there is a centrally-imposed curriculum, the core may be seen as infringing the professional autonomy of teachers. In others, the teaching profession may resist attempts to abolish or reduce the core on the grounds that they would thereby be open to even more public criticism than they are at present. Schools are frequently attacked for devoting too much time to the frills while neglecting the essentials. At the crudest level, this attack takes the form of a simple slogan "back to the basics", that is, the notion that the curriculum should be confined to the fundamental skills of reading, writing, and arithmetic. But there are more sophisticated, and more educationally respectable, versions of the argument in favour of a core curriculum[3].

It is important to bear in mind that no version of the core curriculum is value free. The kinds of knowledge, skills, and values that are considered to be important can rarely be completely uncontroversial. In other words, in order to produce a list of curriculum priorities a set of anterior criteria is a prerequisite. This means that the composition of the core is not universal and immutable but will be different from country to country or region to region within countries and will differ over time as priorities are reordered.

There are at least three important features of the development of the idea of a core curriculum that call for analysis: *i)* the theoretical justification for varying definitions of the core; *ii)* the current trend to specify or to redefine national curricula precisely in terms of a common core rather than segregated and stratified curricula; *iii)* the scope of the core. As to the first, much of the fundamental thinking about the curriculum in terms of a core was carried out in the United States in the late 1950s and early 1960s at the University of Illinois[4]. The model put forward derives a core curriculum from the demands of the culture and economy (vocation, citizenship, and self-cultivation), the uses of knowledge, and a set of learning processes including teaching and learning styles and strategies. Although there is no nation-wide agreement on common core curriculum in the United States, the work of Broudy, Burnett and Smith has been influential there and elsewhere. Many of the national reform reports that have been a feature of United States education during the past decade have argued for a broad core of studies for all youth and have sketched their outlines of what this should comprise[5].

The second feature can be related to the trend in a number of countries to define a core of studies for ever higher levels of schooling. Norway and Sweden were early examples of the attempt to include all secondary as well as primary students and France has recently moved in that direction for the early years of secondary schooling. England, however, officially accepted comprehensive secondary schools in most areas before defining an appropriate comprehensive core curriculum; only since the mid-1970s have attempts been made there to reach national consensus on curriculum planning. The underlying issue in all cases concerns the duration of the core in the entire school cycle. In other words, where should it stop or should it stop at all?

The third feature concerns the scope of the core or proportion of the total curriculum that it should comprise. Should it be so many prescribed hours — say, two-thirds or four-fifths or more of the timetable? If it occupies too large a proportion of school time, will it not stifle teacher initiatives, reduce student options, especially at higher secondary levels, and lead to the disappearance of some desirable subjects, for example Latin and Greek, or design? Each education system needs to strike a reasonable balance between national, regional or local prescription and latitude for flexibility at the school level.

When a society makes education compulsory, then it should acknowledge its responsibility to define what the compensating advantages of that schooling are in terms of a specified curriculum. We come to take the compulsion for granted through familiarity and through general agreement that children and youngsters should attend school. There must nevertheless be visible benefit for what is in fact a loss of freedom.

CURRICULUM CONTENT

Selecting from culture

Having discussed general features of the notion of "core", it is time to address the kind of core curriculum that is to be offered. At the primary level this tends not to pose a problem since there the core principle has long been taken for granted. At the secondary level, however, it can cause very difficult problems. When secondary schools were changing from elitist to more open establishments, it was necessary to design a more broadly-based curriculum for all young people, not simply a revamped version of the old grammar school type. "Watered-down" versions of that curriculum were not an acceptable educational solution for the majority of the population, though the desire to ensure equality of opportunity for all made the pull towards this type of offering often difficult to resist. If it is resisted, however, what should take its place without jeopardising equality of opportunity? Up to the present time, no country has completely solved the problem of providing a suitable curriculum at the secondary level for all levels of abilities in all social groups. When critics of schooling question current standards and quality, this difficulty should be frankly recognised as a central issue.

It should also be recognised that the traditional grammar school, *lycée*, or *Gymnasium* curriculum was by no means ideal even for middle-class students of high ability. The students did not complain very much, however, and thus the system *appeared* to be functioning effectively. The traditional secondary curriculum was becoming less appropriate even for the academic, elite minority long before the 1980s, partly because of its neglect of practical and applied, as opposed to theoretical, studies, and partly because it failed to deal with social and moral development together with an understanding of modern society.

The move away from a heavily cognitive to a more broadly-based curriculum has led to a planning approach that has been described as "selection from culture". Stenhouse made explicit an intention to provide all young people with the kind of "general studies" to which all should have access, especially in the humanities[6]. Lawton has used the technique of cultural analysis to generate a secondary curriculum for all based on eight cultural systems: Socio-political, Economic, Communication, Rationality, Technology, Morality, Belief, Aesthetic[7]. This approach is not meant to displace existing school subjects, but rather to put them into a wider cultural perspective and to provide a rational means of selecting from the culture. Cultural analysis provides a method of comparing the school curriculum with aspects of "culture" in order to identify gaps, mismatches, and contradictions in the education service.

Aspects of this approach can be seen in official United Kingdom documents on curriculum such as those produced by Her Majesty's Inspectorate (HMI)[8]. This view of the curriculum has been very important in the development of school-based curriculum planning in England in the early 1980s. A series of circulars was sent from the Department of Education and Science requiring local education authorities and schools to specify their curricula more carefully in terms of objectives. An approach frequently adopted was to employ the HMI model of "Areas of Experience" as a means of comparing the existing curriculum with a more comprehensive alternative.

The HMI model was designed specifically as a common core curriculum for secondary pupils aged 11-16. It was a considered alternative to the pattern that prevailed in the 1960s and 1970s, namely a "core plus options" design where the emphasis was on options rather than core; a pattern criticised in the United States for being a "cafeteria curriculum", that is, having free choice but paying little attention to "dietary" needs. In 1977, HMI published a report which was extremely critical of options schemes which led to the neglect of the core (the core being expressed in terms of those areas of experience that all young people should have adequate access to before leaving school). This common core curriculum was later referred to as an "entitlement" curriculum, thus conveying the message that all young people had a right to certain worthwhile activities. The "Areas of Experience", as modified in 1985, comprise the following: Aesthetic and creative, Human and social, Linguistic and literary, Mathematical, Moral, Physical, Scientific, Spiritual, Technological. The main idea behind the nine "Areas of Experience" is that at national, regional, and school levels the curriculum should be planned to ensure adequate coverage of each area for all young people.

In several OECD countries, subjects continue to dominate the curriculum as a means of "delivery", but it is now less common for subjects to be seen as goals in their own right which can be taken for granted. Increasingly, subjects have to be justified as means to an end rather than ends in themselves. Teachers are expected to ask "Why are we teaching x but not y?", a necessary step towards reflecting upon the quality of what they teach. Single-subject lessons are, therefore, no longer the only means of reaching the kind of objectives spelt out under the headings of "Areas of Experience" or "Cultural Systems". Modules, sometimes of an interdisciplinary structure, are tending to supplement or displace subjects, though rapid summaries of trends across OECD countries can lead to distortion. Some countries, such as the Netherlands, are returning to a more subject-dominated curriculum, though this does not mean simply turning the clock back to previous practice.

One essential feature of a module is that it is of a more limited duration than the whole school year, lasting, for example, for two afternoons a week for ten weeks. Some modules are designed to be "appetisers" or "tasters", that is, encouraging students to try a new subject for a limited period without long-term commitment for one or two years. That is wise because one of the criticisms of options or cafeteria designs has been that students choose without having adequate knowledge about what they are choosing. More usually, modules are alternatives within a subject area. An advantage of the module pattern is that within a subject area or area of experience specific interests can be catered for which still make a general contribution to the subject as a whole, provided that the overall objectives are clearly planned. For example, schools may offer modules within science on topics ranging from photography, dyes and dyeing to health and hygiene. So long as the scientific objectives are clear, it is not necessary for all pupils to cover exactly the same content. The quality of the learning can thus be improved by means of the use of a modular structure, partly because individual motivation is noticeably improved and partly because much more ground can be thoroughly covered in a comparatively short space of time.

There is no necessary contradiction between the idea of a common core curriculum and giving individual students the opportunity of choosing from a variety of modules. Such a curriculum design can be effectively based on the principle that there may be several equally valid routes into the common curriculum. One of the important functions of schools is to provide students with adequate guidance when making their choices: teachers have a duty to negotiate a balanced curriculum; choice does not have to be unrestrained.

Nevertheless, it cannot be pretended that all curricular tensions and dilemmas evaporate upon close scrutiny and reflection. There does seem to be a tension between a common core for all, usually grounded on some theory of general education, the vocationally-inspired drive towards practical and useful knowledge and skills, and the call to cater for the specific needs and interests of diverse student groups.

Relevance

Whether heard from employers or from young people themselves, a common charge laid at the doors of the school curriculum across OECD countries is that it is insufficiently "relevant". But relevant to what and to whom? The youngster who feels that school knowledge is inappropriate for adolescent mentalities and preoccupations is no doubt drawing on a different notion of "relevance" from that of an employer concerned that young candidates for a job are now ill-equipped for useful work. Neither is likely to argue that the school curriculum should be reduced predominantly to scientific and technical studies even though that is what is commonly invoked as characteristic of greater "relevance".

However the concept of relevance be interpreted, especially in the face of rapid economic change, it has to be recognised that a perfect match between education and manpower needs is neither possible nor desirable because of the wider roles which education must play in developing a responsible and self-renewing citizenry in democratic societies. The challenge can be posed to the education system in terms of finding the "golden mean" — that is, neither over-responding nor under-responding to labour market and economic needs. Specifying where the line of the "golden mean" should be drawn will involve attention to social skills and attitudinal development no less than to specific knowledge and occupational fields. A wide-ranging survey of a number of OECD countries[9] has recently argued that the former are frequently a priority for many employers:

"One of the most significant findings to emerge from this study is the stress being placed especially by employers upon those aspects of the curriculum which are not necessarily cognitive or instrumental. It is evident that employers value these behavioural characteristics as highly as they do the cognitive outcomes of schooling".

Greater economic "relevance" may well also involve the development of active exchanges between schools and local enterprises and employers. It will almost certainly necessitate genuine careers education and advice for all that is given proper status alongside the other purposes of schooling.

Work-oriented and practical studies

A key specific issue here concerns the appropriate balance between general and work-oriented studies. If preparation for working life is treated as a high priority, as it is today in all OECD countries, it is evident that it should illuminate in some way the core curriculum. This may well mean, for example, that all should learn something about the nature of economic and social organisation, master some practical skills, and, wherever possible, visit industrial and commercial enterprises. In addition, those students who plan to leave school at the earliest opportunity should follow optional courses related to their career choices at the earliest opportunity. As we have seen, however, school systems have not always been very successful in devising appropriate curricula for this group.

When preparation for working life is treated as an integral part of the core curriculum, the vexed issue of reconciling general and vocational education may be resolved. The task of determining how much and what sort of vocational education there should be remains. On the one hand, it is a disadvantage for those who intend to continue their formal education to a further stage to have to spend too much time on vocational studies directly related to immediate employment; on the other hand, those intending to leave at the end of compulsory schooling are often only really motivated when they study vocational subjects. One solution appears to lie in the flexible provision of optional studies outside the core curriculum designed to cater for these two interest groups and in interpreting education for working life in a broad sense. As underlined several times, the curriculum extends beyond specific subject matter to embrace pedagogy and the organisation of learning. Non-traditional subject matter cannot be successfully taught and learned using only traditional methods. Broadening the academic curriculum means broadening the nature and ambit of schooling.

The current emphasis on economic ends has required rethinking of the old "general/vocational" distinction. General education should include teaching and guidance about working life and training requirements in different occupations, the mechanics of the labour market and of collective bargaining, and the role of major industries in the national economy. As to useful "employable skills", the ones commonly mentioned by those who argue that schools should prepare pupils better for working life accord well with what schools seek to develop anyway: literacy, the ability to communicate orally, numeracy, manual and mental dexterity, how to co-operate with others, the habits of hard effort — as well as with the universally acclaimed and lofty aim of "learning to learn". No doubt, "independent critical thinking" also makes young persons valuable and productive in places of employment. It would be a sad reflection on working life if this were not so. How far these aims are compatible with a limited emphasis on "basics" is far from clear. The foundation on which criticisms of schools, teaching, and teachers rest needs thus to be clarified and priorities decided; engendering critical mastery may involve radical departures from traditional notions of what schooling and classrooms are rather than a return to previous practice.

OBJECTIVES AND EVALUATION

Curriculum planning and objectives

The use of objectives in curriculum planning, at different levels — national, regional, school, classroom — can be a constructive way of raising standards of achievement simply by focusing clearly on certain areas and by linking evaluation with teaching. It can never be assumed, however, that the existing objectives of a school system are the right ones. What may be required is a significant shift of objectives.

In his influential book *Basic Principles of Curriculum and Instruction*, Tyler[10] described curriculum planning as a simple linear model: aims and objectives—content—organisation—evaluation. The model can be interpreted in two ways: either as a means of clarifying teachers' intentions and instructional methods or as a dogmatic assertion of the only way curriculum should be designed. The first interpretation offers a fruitful approach; the second interpretation, reinforced by behaviourist psychology, can trivialise the teaching/learning process and lead to a pedagogy based on tick schedules.

Education is not a closed system of right answers. Teachers cannot always specify in advance exactly how each student should respond as a result of a teaching/learning programme. They may be able to do so when the teaching programme is concerned with skills or factual information. However, detailed specification becomes dangerously inapplicable when associated with the more abstract and qualitative aspects of knowledge and values. For example, in the field of foreign languages the behavioural objectives model may be helpful at the level of learning vocabulary or verb endings, but if the real goal is to introduce students to another country's culture through the world of literature, then the students' responses cannot be predicted. There is no one correct way of interpreting a poem by Hugo or Whitman, Cervantès' *Don Quixote*, or Goethe's *Faust*. There is no one right answer to a question such as "Discuss the origins of the First World War", although there are certainly wrong answers. To attempt to predict the correct response would be to limit the range of thought in a way that is anti-educational.

However, as Skilbeck[1] has pointed out, if we move the meaning of objectives away from the behavioural model and its connotations of complete prespecification, then the idea of objectives as purposes or goals can be very helpful:

"Sometimes it is argued that the objectives model infers measurable outcomes (things learnt), whereas the process model specifies contexts, conditions, criteria and activities in learning. There is value in this distinction, but it is erroneous to suggest that the objectives model is necessarily coupled with prespecified, measurable, specific items (facts, concepts, skills) or to imply that ascertainable outcomes are not important in discussing learning processes." (page 210)

Curriculum planning and evaluation

In Chapter 7, the issues of assessment, appraisal, and monitoring will be considered in wider terms. Here, the concern is with the strict relationship between curriculum planning and evaluation at the school level. One of the benefits claimed for a curriculum design which incorporates elements of the objectives model is that aims and evaluation are brought much closer together. The desirability of this relationship might seem obvious. Yet one of the most common criticisms of schooling in most countries is the lack of clear links between the two. In many countries, terminal examinations have tended to dictate the curriculum rather than serving as one form of assessment. Indeed, they can dominate the teaching/learning process rather than simply indicating how effective it is.

An even more serious criticism of undue reliance on terminal examinations is that, as Bruner once observed, it is like waiting until a war is over before creating an intelligence service. In other words, it is vital that evaluation should be formative as well as summative. The trouble with relying on end-of-course examinations is that however useful the results may be to employers and other outsiders, it is too late to put right any deficiencies in an individual's or a group's learning programme. Evaluation must be a carefully planned combination of formative (continuous) assessment and summative (terminal) judgements. A significant aspect of formative evaluation is its diagnostic function. *It is essential not only to identify what a student does not understand, but also to attempt to discover the source of the misunderstanding so that it can be remedied.* Although crucial in any endeavour to improve the quality of teaching and learning, the diagnostic role of the teacher is often neglected to a surprising extent in curriculum planning.

Today it is increasingly recognised that to allow a student's work for a whole year or more to be summarised as a single grade is not only inadequate as a form of assessment but is also unhelpful from a pedagogic point of view. Accordingly, end-of-course written examinations are being supplemented, and sometimes replaced, by more comprehensive records of continuous achievement which present a profile of abilities and achievements instead of a single grade or a mark of pass or fail. This interpretation of evaluation is not simply a more efficient way of recording progress since it also represents a different approach to considering educational achievement. Studies of motivation have shown for many years the need to give frequent and positive feedback to learners. Continuous record-keeping and assessment are closely connected with curriculum planning; if a pupil's progress through a course or programme is being plotted or monitored at regular intervals, it must be related to a planned sequence or development in the programme itself. Thus curriculum and evaluation are brought together at the planning stage as well as when the student is assessed. The course is likely to be broken down into stages, possibly modules, where certain kinds of learning should have taken place; assessment is appropriate at all such points.

Frequent feedback of information about performance is necessary for all students, and crucial for those students who lack confidence in their ability in a particular part of the curriculum. It is unwarranted to label such students as "less able" or "backward" since teachers' assumptions about ability are often much too simple and stereotyped. As Hargreaves[11] reports:

> "Most teachers have little personal experience of systematic failure; as pupils they were almost always relatively successful — though they are anxious to tell us they were rebels in their own way. Some, like me, have a skeleton or two in their academic cupboard. I was not successful during my schooldays at woodwork. Slowly I grew to dislike and then to hate the subject at which I was failing; and so, not surprisingly, what few skills I had deteriorated rapidly. Soon I was the target of teacher criticism. 'Everyone stop work', the teacher would announce, 'and look at Hargreaves'. I knew I was to be the exemplar of what not to be doing " (page 63).

Valuable lessons emerge from this anecdotal example: the need to assess achievement positively whenever possible — not to ignore failure but to try to remedy it; the limited view of "ability" which distorts the educational process in many schools and too often prevails. Differentiation is necessary but needs to be based on more complex models than unidimensional notions of ability; there is also the desirability of allowing students to choose within a core curriculum, according to taste and interest, irrespective of their ability. A narrow view of curriculum results in some schools assessing educational development according to restricted criteria.

Many schools have begun to move away from terminal examinations, whether internally or externally administered, as the main form of assessment and are looking for a battery of techniques for assessing pupils continuously. Graded tests, criterion-referenced examinations, and profiling systems are all useful in this respect but they can involve dangers that teachers and planners should be more aware of and each is discussed in turn below.

Graded tests have become fashionable in certain educational circles in OECD countries. It is argued that they have a history of success in music, for example, which could be applied to other subject areas. In music, students progress from one grade to the next, irrespective of age, according to performance judged by established public standards. Recently attempts have been made to apply graded testing to a number of other subjects such as mathematics and modern languages. Some advantages have been reported, but two dangers emerge, that are not unconnected with the arguments employed above about behavioural objectives. The first danger lies in the assumption that because a curriculum design strategy works well within one subject area or at one level, the advantages are generally transferable to the whole curriculum whereas in this case they may or may not be, and the probability is that there are limitations. Second, graded tests have a restricted range: they are much better suited to lower-level skills than to complex issues of interpretation or evaluation. Graded tests are also restricted in the sense that they can rarely be used diagnostically, the emphasis being on performance and achievement instead of remedying gaps or misunderstandings. Graded tests certainly have a place in a rationally planned evaluation scheme, but they will not solve all the problems confronted in raising achievement in education and the ever-present danger of teaching to the test needs to be counteracted.

Criterion-referenced tests or examinations: the advantages of criterion-referencing have often been proclaimed in recent years compared with norm-referenced tests and examinations. Yet, caution is called for. With a norm-referenced test, individuals are judged not by their own improved performance, but in comparison with the performance of all the others taking the test. Their marks are compared with the average, and the result declared to be good or bad in relation to that average. But, to take an extreme example, a candidate might be at the top of a group where the overall standard was so poor that that individual's standard is in absolute terms actually low. Thus, one way of maintaining or raising standards that has been spotted by politicians and planners is to specify standards or criteria that every student should reach.

The best-known example of criterion-referencing is the driving test, where a range of competences is specified, and every candidate must pass all of them in order to succeed. There are significant advantages in this method. Criterion-referencing when applied to some parts of the curriculum is likely to improve results when:

— The criteria of success are clear to the student and to the examiner;
— The emphasis is on the learner's individual performance and not on the relation of that performance to others;
— Coverage of curriculum subject matter can be carefully related to criteria for testing;
— The diagnosis of learning difficulties is facilitated;
— Criteria can be graded for difficulty and related to levels of understanding.

At the same time, several qualifications are needed to any general endorsement of criterion-referencing. First, it is appropriate for assessing skills, but not universally applicable in education. It is, for example, easier to specify the skills needed to be a competent driver than the qualities needed to be a good historian or physicist. Second is the related point that some aspects of education have to do with judgement rather than simple criteria. For example, in those areas of the curriculum concerned with moral education or personal and social development, judgement is more appropriate than prespecified criteria. Third, all criterion-referencing includes an element of norm-referencing. To return to the simple example of the driving test, it would be foolish to pretend that all examiners operate with exactly the same standards of pass/fail or that notions of adequacy are not in some way informed by what others achieve. One examiner might pass a candidate with a performance which another examiner would fail — even the same examiner may not be totally consistent. All criteria include aspects of examiner norms, and the driving test as a whole encapsulates a set of normative judgements about what is considered to be a competent driver in a particular society at a particular time.

Good curriculum design brings aims and evaluation close together. The essential need is to assess achievement positively whenever possible — not to ignore failure but to try to remedy it. Graded tests have a place in a rationally planned evaluation scheme. Criterion-referenced tests or examinations have certain advantages; in particular, they make it possible to specify standards or criteria that every student should reach.

Profiles and profiling systems: reference has just been made to the inadequacy of terminal examinations as a single means of assessment. Profiles have recently gained currency as a superior alternative. However, the word "profile" can be used with two quite different meanings. In contrast to a written examination which assesses only one aspect of a school subject, profiles are sometimes advocated as a way of indicating performance across a range of skills or knowledge; whereas a written examination produces a single mark or grade, a profile can generate a range of comments or marks across the whole subject area. The second meaning of profile is to indicate not a way of assessing a subject but a means of expressing assessment across the whole curriculum. The essence of profiling is that it covers a wide area either within a subject or over a number of subjects, preferably using a variety of assessment procedures, oral as well as written, skills as well as knowledge, processes as well as memorisation and so on.

The potential advantages of profiles and profiling systems are clear, while some problems remain and certain others are created by their use. The major problem concerns the intended reader of the profile. If it is aimed at employers, then they are likely to demand objectivity rather than teacher judgement, thus limiting the range of possible techniques. If the profile is designed for students and their parents, then greater flexibility is possible, provided that some effort has been made to explain its purpose. One advantage claimed for certain kinds of profiling systems is the value of student self-assessment, but this too is likely to be ruled out if the major purpose of the profile is for job selection or selection into the next stage of education. Profiling is most valuable when used as a means of assessing performance across the whole curriculum.

Evaluation of the curriculum itself

So far, evaluation has been considered in terms of assessing student learning in the school, but there are other essential kinds of evaluation associated with curriculum planning, including the evaluation of the whole process of curriculum design and implementation. Part of curriculum planning is the incorporation of evaluation into the first stage of the plan rather than as an afterthought. One purpose of evaluation is to monitor the quality of the curriculum offered at each stage of the implementation process. The first stage is clearly to ensure that the general purpose of the curriculum is manifest and translated into valid objectives. A secondary, but essential, role for curriculum evaluation is to monitor the effectiveness of the teaching/learning process. Teachers should have a full perception of aims and objectives and the ability to transform these into effective work plans, bearing in mind the needs of individual pupils. Teachers also need to command the techniques of guidance and negotiation with students. The monitoring of learning should be concerned with general problems of motivation, including the balance between immediate interests and long-term needs; vocational interests are important but should not be allowed to dominate student choices or be translated into too specific vocational training.

A major problem, already referred to above, is concerned with the difficulty of managing the tension between the need for a core curriculum and the desirability of students having the opportunity to make choices. There is no necessary contradiction here but a real difficulty to be overcome, partly by individual teachers and partly by the structure and organisation of the curriculum. It is important to write into the plan *options* or choices *within* the core rather than assuming that choices are only possible as alternatives to the core.

CONCLUSIONS: CURRICULUM PLANNING TO RAISE QUALITY

The role of curriculum planning in improving the quality of schooling has been neglected in most OECD countries. This may seem surprising given that many countries have a well-defined national curriculum. But a highly-centralised and detailed published curriculum does not necessarily ensure the desired outcomes. Neither is the policy of leaving all curricular decisions to individual schools a satisfactory alternative solution. Many OECD countries are, therefore, now working towards a careful balance between centrally-negotiated national guidelines and school-based planning for curriculum implementation. Achieving that balance is by no means easy, and the specific problems will differ from one country to another according to the historical development of educational tradition.

Curriculum planning, nationally and locally, must operate according to an *a priori* theory. Most societies, consciously or unconsciously, seem to be working with some kind of curriculum theory in mind based on "social and individual needs". It would improve the curriculum planning machinery if these underlying values were to be made more explicit, perhaps by a conscious programme of specification such as cultural analysis. One of the current recipes for improving the quality of the curriculum is to demand that it be "broad, balanced, relevant, and differentiated". Each of these adjectives, however, conceals several difficulties. *Broad* and *balanced* are both words that indicate general approval, but they are meaningless unless a clear indication is given about the territory to be covered and the ingredients which are to be balanced. In other words, both these terms should indicate a prior commitment to some kind of theory of a tenable curriculum. Very often this fundamental requirement is taken for granted. A major contribution towards improving the quality of the curriculum can be made by making explicit the underlying purposes of education, and then by determining how they can be realised in classroom practice.

Similarly, the meaning of *relevant* is not immediately transparent, as we have seen. It is often used to indicate work-oriented curriculum, but there are other kinds of relevance which ought to be included within a well-planned curriculum; for example, that knowledge is built up in ways that enable the student to see and understand how the parts fit together. Lack of relevance is also used to criticise curricula which are unduly academic and therefore not susceptible to practical application for the majority. This is an important aspect of curriculum planning, but it needs to be spelt out carefully rather than simply labelled.

Finally, *differentiation* can also be interpreted in a variety of ways. A narrow way is to suggest that the curriculum must cater for all levels of ability without stratification, but that is only one kind of difference with which curriculum planners ought to be concerned. Intelligence is obviously an important individual difference but there are many others that have implications for teaching and learning styles such as those of motivation and application. Gender differences in approaches to learning also deserve close attention.

Other problems of curriculum planning include cultural lag and curriculum inertia: educational institutions, as is well known, tend to respond less quickly to social change than many other institutions. That is both inevitable and reasonable. Education is necessarily tradition-oriented to some degree and there are some features of modern society which are anti-educational and should be resisted. But many schools also tend to be resistant to changes of any kind. In order to be able to discriminate between desirable and undesirable change, some form of curriculum theory, including criteria for reacting to change, is therefore essential.

Teachers need to be trained in such a way as to enable them to translate curriculum aims or national guidelines into operational classroom objectives and schemes of work. Curriculum planning, national and local, is a continuous process of improvement and adaptation. It is obvious that teachers need good initial training and regular updating by means of in-service education. But obvious though this need is to state, it is arguable that curriculum policies and teacher policies are too often divorced — that each belongs to its own departments and specialists. Curriculum planning, instead, needs to write in teacher competences, supply, and training needs from the outset. What is, perhaps, even less obvious is that teachers also require adequate time for the process of curriculum planning within the school. Occasionally, major innovations such as the introduction of computers into schools will call for substantial expenditure on retraining programmes. Professional teachers need to be able to articulate the general aims of education and of their school in a meaningful way to students, parents, and others outside the school system. Each school must devote time and care to formulating its own goals and methods within the national guidelines.

One of the dangers that national and school curriculum planning must counteract is the tendency for educational institutions to become dominated by their assessment techniques. Examinations and tests should be teachers' servants and not their masters. Teachers must be competent to resist technocratic-bureaucratic domination by asserting their own proven assessment practices as well as be willing to adopt new techniques. Likewise teachers must be able not only to see curriculum as a whole, but also to break it down into smaller units or modules for teaching and evaluating purposes. Frequent feedback to students, giving realistic but positive assessment, is essential.

Teachers should be constantly developing and improving techniques of comprehensive record-keeping as part of the process of planning and evaluation of the curriculum. One increasingly important aspect of the teacher's role is to guide students' choices and to negotiate teaching/learning contracts with them. In this way the teacher-student relationship can become much more productive, and the student will be motivated to play a more active part in learning, curriculum planning at the individual level and self-assessment. Good teachers capitalise on the motivation of students, who nearly always wish to enter the labour market well prepared, but it is dishonest and counter-productive to pretend that the only purpose of the curriculum is to prepare young people for work. A balanced approach to preparation for the whole of adult life is an indispensable feature of a well-planned curriculum.

A common core curriculum is not necessarily a uniform curriculum. A key element in the art of curriculum planning is to provide a variety of routes *into* important areas of knowledge, skills and values, as well as different exit routes which can develop individual interests and abilities to the highest possible levels. Some planning of this kind for differentiation can take place nationally, but it is likely to be most effective when it is planned and implemented at the school level in relation to specific individual and group needs for differentiation.

NOTES AND REFERENCES

1. Skilbeck. M. (1984), *School-Based Curriculum Development*, Harper and Row, London.
2. Rousseau, J.J. (1762), *Emile*, London (Everyman edn. 1911).
3. OECD (1983), *Compulsory Schooling in a Changing World*, Paris.
4. Broudy, H.S., Smith, B.O., and Burnett, J.R. (1964), *Democracy and Excellence in American Secondary Education*, Rand McNally, Chicago, Illinois.
5. From the early wave of reform proposals see in particular National Commission on Excellence in Education (1983), *A Nation at Risk* (revised title: *The Imperative for Educational Reform*), United States Department of Education, Washington D.C.; Boyer, E. (1983), *High School: A Report on Secondary Education in America*, Harper and Row, New York; Adler, M.J. (1983), *The Paideia Proposal*, MacMillan, New York; College Entrance Examination Board (1983), *Academic Preparation for College: What Students Need to Know and Be Able to Do*, New York.
6. Stenhouse, L. (1975), *An Introduction to Curriculum Research and Development*, Heinemann, London.
7. Lawton, D. (1983), *Curriculum Studies and Educational Planning*, Hodder and Stoughton Educational, London.
8. See, for example, Department of Education and Science (1977), *Curriculum 11-16*, HMSO, London; Department of Education and Science (1985), *The Curriculum from 5 to 16*, HMSO, London.
9. Beare, H. and Lemke, H. (1987), "The Curriculum and the Economy" (OECD internal document).
10. Tyler, R. (1949), *Basic Principles of Curriculum and Instruction*, University of Chicago Press, Illinois.
11. Hargreaves, D. (1982), *The Challenge for the Comprehensive School: Culture, Curriculum, and Community*, Routledge and Kegan Paul, London, Boston, and Henley.

Chapter 5

THE VITAL ROLE OF TEACHERS

TEACHERS AND QUALITY

In 1983, the OECD Report *Compulsory Schooling in a Changing World* made the following statement about the challenges and difficulties today facing teachers:

"Given the advent of falling enrolments and increasing pressures for changes in the curriculum and the governance of schools it will be particularly difficult during the next decade to maintain the morale and competence of the teaching force. Many teachers may find themselves under double stress. On the one hand, they will naturally feel disturbed if there are cutbacks to recruitment, blocks on promotion and talk of competency tests and redundancies in the air. On the other hand, they will be exposed to increasing pressure to diversify their functions, to modify their teaching styles, to cope with new curricular demands, and to relinquish some of their long-established autonomy.

For this reason it will be necessary to ensure that all initial teacher training courses have sufficient depth, scope and flexibility to respond quickly and effectively to changes in the schools, for example the use of micro-instructional techniques and the adoption of team-teaching. It will be equally necessary to expand and to improve the provision for professional development through in-service training so as to enable established teachers to keep up to date and to adapt to all the new demands being made upon them. Recent experiments indicate that in-service training is most effective when courses in universities or training institutions are wedded to the application of theory in the schools. School-based training appears to be particularly effective".[1]

Then, in 1984, the OECD Ministers of Education gave a clear priority to the need to reassess teaching conditions and policies with a view to enhancing school performance:

"Effective schooling at all levels depends on a highly qualified and motivated teaching force. The tasks of teachers are today more complex and demanding than in the past. They have to respond to the wishes of parents regarding educational outcomes, the social need for wider access to education, and pressures for more democratic participation within the schools. The recruitment, working conditions and the training of teachers, as well as their status, incentives and career prospects, need to be re-examined".[2]

Everyone agrees that the competence and commitment of teachers are a vital prerequisite for producing an education of quality. Yet in many OECD countries at the present time there is public discontent with the performance of teachers and many teachers are manifestly unhappy with their lot. Why is this so? The discontent comes from the feeling that some teachers are not properly equipped professionally or personally to meet the new tasks and challenges posed in the classroom. As for teacher dissatisfaction, it arises from a loss of self-esteem which is, in turn, connected with a sense of declining social status and conditions of service that are felt to be unsatisfactory.

What is to be done? A four-pronged approach is called for:

- *i)* Attract good recruits;
- *ii)* Prepare the new teacher more effectively;
- *iii)* Take measures to maintain the competence of practising teachers;
- *iv)* Generally seek to raise teacher morale and motivation.

These aims are easy to state but difficult to adopt. Each will be considered in turn.

ATTRACTING GOOD RECRUITS

It is frequently stated that during the years of educational expansion in the 1960s and 1970s many teachers were appointed who were not properly qualified either academically or in pedagogical skills. That is a problem to be addressed in part by In-Service Education and Training (INSET) which will be discussed in the next section. What is disturbing in at least some countries today is the fact that some recruits to *initial* teacher training continue to be of low academic calibre or poorly motivated towards a teaching career. Problems arise because the teaching force must be replenished from a limited pool of talent in competition, which is often fierce, with other professions as well as with industrial and commercial firms. It also arises from the related fact that the overwhelming majority of recruits continue to come straight from colleges and universities. More mature candidates with experience from another form of life should no doubt be encouraged to take up teaching.

Many able young people will only be attracted to teaching as a career if pay and conditions of service are reasonably attractive. Opinions differ about how important an inducement salaries are. Some insist that unless teachers are well paid, recruitment problems will remain unsolved. Others believe that teaching will continue to attract sufficient numbers of good quality applicants, despite low pay, provided that conditions of service are congenial, that teaching is regarded as a worthwhile occupation, and that there are reasonable prospects for personal satisfaction within the profession. Inquiries about incentives certainly show a high rating for non-pecuniary factors. But low pay does tend to lead to low status. Thus, although some people will always be attracted to teaching for other than financial reasons, there is almost certainly a salary limit below which many potential candidates will be reluctant to apply, especially if public authorities adopt anything like an adversarial stance in salary negotiations. The correlation between financial rewards and status, on the one hand, and the quality of recruits to teaching, on the other, cannot be ignored, even though it is hard to pinpoint with evidence. The phenomenon is not simply the short-term reaction to marginal differences in salaries but the long-term relationship between professional status, public perceptions, and societal reward.

At the same time, it becomes even more difficult than in the past to regard teaching as having the same kind of professional clout as medicine or law. There are simply too many teachers in each country for them to be accorded the elite status possessed by a few other professional groups. Teachers are also too numerous to be able to command comparatively high salaries, since their emoluments already account for around 80 per cent of the educational budget in most Member countries. The appeal to would-be recruits, therefore, must largely rest on the overall attractiveness of teaching as a career, taking all factors into account.

Many countries have experienced a dramatic fall in numbers of pupils in primary and secondary schools since the late 1970s and consequently a decline in the demand for teachers. Such a situation ought to make it possible to operate a more selective recruitment policy without increasing costs. In practice, education authorities have frequently made other choices. Coombs[3] shows that many OECD countries have taken advantage of the improved teacher supply to provide special services to handicapped children and to enrich educational services in such subjects as art and music, which is, of course, all to the good. In some countries, schools in "problem neighbourhoods" have been allocated additional teachers, which is also perfectly justified. Moreover, a surplus of teacher supply often carries with it unfortunate side-effects, declining job prospects in teaching deterring potential candidates from applying, and there are accordingly fewer candidates to choose from.

Given these factors, a clear conception of the qualities to be expected of a good teacher and a very positive selection policy are required if full advantage is to be taken of falling enrolments. Realising this, some countries have seized the opportunity to replace unqualified or underqualified by well-qualified teachers (though, as discussed below, academic qualifications alone are not a sufficient condition of being a good teacher). The particular difficulty sometimes remains of finding appropriately qualified candidates in such subjects as mathematics and physics. Most professional associations frown on the overt practice of paying higher salaries to teachers of scarce subjects, particularly if they have lower qualification levels than their colleagues in subjects where there is a relative surplus. So, some education authorities are obliged either to employ poorly-qualified teachers of certain subjects or to pay all teachers more in order to attract those who would otherwise be lured into non-teaching occupations.

The general rule ought to be to select candidates not only with the best possible academic qualifications but also with desirable attitudes and personality traits. The positive correlation between good academic qualifications and a beneficial effect on pupil learning is not remarkably high. Successful teaching is primarily due to personality characteristics such as patience, persistence, the ability to analyse problems and empathy with students. Yet very few training institutions or colleges seriously attempt to select future teachers according to personality in any way that could be described as scientific, or even systematic and they may be under pressure to relax such selection as does occur when few candidates apply.

Many training establishments interview all candidates for places on initial training courses, and some of them would claim to use the interview to identify personality traits, but follow-up tends to be weak. In recent years it has been recognised that practising teachers may be at least as successful as teacher trainers in conducting the selection procedure. Experiments have been tried of arranging preliminary interviews in a school setting, and of observing the applicant in contact with children, with a view to obtaining better predictive results[4]. Properly controlled studies are needed to put alternative procedures of this kind to the test. Meanwhile, uncertainty about the effectiveness of specific selection procedures has not prevented some governments from introducing them as official policy.

PREPARING EFFECTIVE TEACHERS

Initial teacher education has always been subject to a good deal of criticism, ranging from allegations — not least from teacher trainees themselves — about low academic standards to lack of relevance to classroom practice. Four desiderata appear to be indispensable:

  i) A correct balance between theory and practice;
  ii) Participation of practising teachers;
  iii) Use of competence-based training;
  iv) Fully qualified teacher educators.

Balance between theory and practice

Rhoades[5] has suggested that in the United States too much attention has been paid to the quality of students entering initial training for teaching and too little to the quality of the courses:

> "In general, more attention and resources have been directed towards input and output factors. The process of teacher education has been relatively ignored. For instance, federal money is used for scholarships to attract academically talented students to teacher education, but there is no funding for institutions to improve the teacher education programmes these students will take".

He goes on to suggest that the basic problem of teacher education is that it finds itself positioned between two worlds — that of higher education and the school. On the one side, teacher education is pulled in the direction of being more academic or more like other academic disciplines; on the other side, teacher education is urged to be more practical, to move close to the real world of the classroom, and to ensure that teacher trainers have recent and relevant experience in schools.

Sometimes these opposing claims are seen in a slightly different way; should the initial training course prepare the student for an entire career in teaching or should it simply offer a survival kit for the first few months backed up by continuing guidance? This choice has often been made more critical by the fact that in many countries teachers regard their initial training as a licence to practise for life and do not willingly seek any in-service education. The result is that, if they are not exposed at this stage to a professional injection of educational philosophy, psychology, and sociology before they qualify, they never will be. Thus, reform of initial teacher education needs to be viewed as part of a larger picture — the total career pattern of a teacher including initial training, induction, professional development, in-service education, and opportunities for taking qualifications such as higher degrees. If initial training is seen in that continuing context, it can be regarded as practical, even school-based, without being devoid of theory.

It is misleading to consider the relation between theory and practice as a process of learning the theory and then putting it into practice. There is an increasing tendency to regard the relation between theory and practice as extremely complex, and to see genuine educational theory as something which arises out of practice, relying to some extent on theoretical insights developed in other disciplines such as philosophy, sociology or psychology. The educational theory that emerges is, however, experience-based rather than a simple amalgam of extracts from other disciplines. The move away from educational theory based on related disciplines to various kinds of problem-centred or practice-centred courses is among the most promising of current developments in education.

Participation of practising teachers

In some countries the notion of "lead teachers" who assume partial responsibility for the training of student teachers is well established. They form a useful bridge between the world of the school and the academic world of the university or college. Their use also provides an additional career route for good teachers who would prefer to remain in the classroom rather than become administrators. Other countries have also developed similar roles for supervising teachers, without using a term such as "master teacher", which is sometimes regarded as inappropriate. But "teacher tutors" who typically spend the majority of their time in their schools and a significant minority of their time in the training institution, are becoming important in several countries.

Competence-based teacher education

The approach to teacher training which has become known as competence- or performance-based teacher education began as a reaction against those university or college courses which were "theoretical" in a way which was regarded by trainers and students as remote from the classroom and irrelevant to the needs of the student teacher. Unfortunately, this healthy reaction against a misconceived view of theory has often developed into an extreme movement. Specific skills of interacting with pupils were spelled out very clearly, and this was very helpful to student teachers, but later the competence-based orthodoxy demanded that nothing but a prespecified list of behavioural objectives could be permitted. Theory was thus not abolished but was replaced by a very narrow theory of learning derived from behaviourist psychology. The main danger of that approach is that the teacher's role becomes a very mechanical one and does not permit the teacher or student teacher to adopt a reflective attitude towards the purpose of what he or she is trying to achieve. Teaching becomes oversimplified and completely identified with instruction. No distinction between education and training is made.

But there is value in the competence-based approach as part of initial training so long as it is not taken to extremes. It is useful for teachers to acquire specific classroom skills; it is helpful to spell out clearly what a teacher hopes to achieve in a lesson in terms of knowledge, skills and attitudes; all education involves certain kinds of training procedures[6]. However, education should not be totally identified with training, and professional teachers need to be able to reflect on the education process and to analyse why certain learning experiences are worthwhile.

No doubt initial training establishments should also be rigorous in weeding out trainee teachers with personalities found to be incompatible with school teaching. Part of the initial training problem is that there is simply too much information to acquire and too many skills to learn in the limited time available; initial training, therefore, must be seen as the first stage of professional preparation, not the whole of it.

Capacity of teacher educators

The competence-based movement developed as a reaction against inadequate teacher education programmes. If teacher education is to be improved, it will be essential to maintain and enhance the quality of those directly responsible for it. Taylor[7] and Rhoades have compared those university teachers involved in teacher training with those in other academic subjects; education staff spend less time on research than other university staff and a higher proportion engage in no research; education staff tend to have less good academic degrees from less prestigious universities.

Rhoades discusses the "cost of academic excellence" in England and the United States. In England academic excellence is regarded as rating much greater priority than professional competence; in the United States there is little emphasis on academic excellence, but American students are better prepared professionally. He reports that although British students score higher on intelligence and verbal comprehension tests than American students, they score lower on measures of professional knowledge. He emphasizes that such tests measure knowledge of subject matter not the students' capacity to apply it. Rhoades found no evidence that this knowledge helped students to become more effective teachers. American students were equally critical of the theoretical bias in their courses.

Such findings point to the need to develop different, but equally rigorous, criteria to measure excellence among teacher trainers. They should not simply follow the academic criteria customary in other faculties. It will be necessary for their professional development to be related not only to recent experience of teaching in schools, but with ways of combining educational research, practical work in schools involving students, and the recording of such experience which will be of enduring professional interest as well as personally beneficial in terms of "keeping in touch with the classroom". This will require a broader view of what counts as research in education, and the development of more adequate means of evaluating such practice-based research. They should not be content to be judged in the same way as other academics, although some of them may wish to be, and anyway teacher education is pulled in conflicting directions — to demonstrate vigorous standards alongside other faculties and to provide a practical training for teachers in the classroom. Teacher educators might develop styles of practice and research similar in some respects to the "clinical model" of medical education.

MAINTAINING TEACHER COMPETENCE

It has already been suggested that the problem of teacher quality needs to be seen as a sequential process: recruiting potentially effective teachers; providing effective initial courses; retaining effective teachers in the profession and making the best use of them by continuing professional education and development. This post-initial aspect of teacher education is probably the most important as well as the most neglected in most countries. It will be convenient to sub-divide it into three overlapping phases: induction; in-service education; professional development. The purpose of induction is to continue initial professional preparation into the first year or so of teaching; at the end of this stage, the teacher should be able to strengthen his or her professionalism by means of a variety of in-service courses; subsequently, teachers should be offered preparation for more specific professional roles such as head of department or deputy principal by specialised courses including higher degrees.

Induction

In most countries passing an initial training course is followed by a period of induction or probation — often one year — before fully qualified teacher status is achieved. Issues of certification and induction are thus closely related. Induction into the profession is an important stage of professional development.

In the United Kingdom the Plowden Report (1967) suggested that "it is doubtful if the majority of young teachers are given the conditions and guidance in their first posts which will reinforce their training and lead to rising standards in the profession as a whole". With that deficiency in mind the James Report[8] recommended that during the first year of teaching, the newly qualified teacher should be given a lighter teaching load so that the equivalent of one day each week could be spent on further training, guided by a professional tutor. This has not been applied as national policy in the United Kingdom but some local education authorities have made efforts along those lines to use the first year in the profession as a mixture of useful teaching experience and further professional education. Taylor and Dale[9] surveyed the probationary year in the United Kingdom under six headings:

1. Statutory provisions for probation;
2. Appointment and placement;
3. Experience and problems in the classroom;
4. Experience and problems in the school;
5. The effect on the probationer's personal life;
6. In-service training and assessment.

Practice varies considerably from one country to another. In Sweden, for example, the teacher training committee insists that refresher courses form an integral part of the work of colleges of education. In some countries, inspectors have a special responsibility for overseeing the work of probationary teachers. Inspectors report on them, commenting on their teaching ability and pupils' reactions. In Germany, the beginning teacher has still to sit the second part of the examination for full qualification after anything from 1 to 3 years or more of practical training with "quality control" as a major aspect. In other countries supervision is much less systematic and may amount to no more than informal advice from experienced teachers. In a number of countries, little progress has been made since the 1971 OECD report reviewed practices which were then current[10].

In-service education

In-service education and training of teachers (INSET) are regarded as a very high priority in most OECD countries. At a time of declining pupil numbers and declining recruitment through initial training the investment in INSET is manifestly the most effective way of improving the quality of teaching generally, especially given the relatively low average age of the teaching force in nearly all countries. Yet INSET has often been neglected in the past both as a means of teacher improvement and a topic for study and evaluation[11]. Even so, as Neave has recently summarised for European countries, that neglect is being increasingly met in the face of a manifest need:

"Indeed, as the number of newly fledged teachers taking up post falls — as it has done over the past half decade in most countries — the price of meeting change in mission and knowledge, skills and qualifications has to be paid by quite massive expansion in this area. Some countries already have in place extensive systems of in-service training. In Denmark, for instance, around 30 per cent of pre-primary school staff attend at least one course per year, whilst, due to limitation on places, only 20 per cent of teachers in the Folkesskole are admitted per year to part-time courses. Other countries, no less ambitious, are gearing up both provision and facilities to deal with a very substantial percentage of their teaching body per year. Italy has set the annual target at 30 per cent of the whole teaching profession participating per annum. Similar priorities are to be seen in France where target figures for teachers undergoing in-service education have been set at 320 000 for the primary sector by 1988 and 300 000 for the secondary sector. Corresponding budgetary commitments under this head have risen by more than three times between 1982 and 1986. Likewise, in the Netherlands, plans envisage some 40 000 teachers undergoing in-service education".[12]

In most OECD countries, as we have already seen, annual intakes of new teachers are very small compared with the number of experienced teachers already working in the schools. If changes and improvements in quality are desired, then the resources devoted to in-service education ought to be much more important than money spent on initial training. In the past, this strategic distinction has not been sufficiently emphasized and comparatively little has been spent on in-service education of teachers.

There is much confusing and conflicting opinion about the provision of in-service courses. On the one hand, it is often stated that teachers are an under-educated and under-trained profession; on the other hand, it appears that, in many countries, some teachers are not eager to attend courses, although they may acknowledge the need for further training and are among those who arguably would benefit most from it. This may not necessarily be a contradiction. Many teachers need much convincing that training courses are not only useful and relevant, but will also benefit them personally and professionally. All too often, apart from the intrinsic interest, there is little incentive for teachers to attend any courses or to upgrade their qualifications. Some spend their own time and their own money on courses without any expectation of tangible reward.

Against this negative background, three reforms appear to be required: first, in-service education should be provided on a more uniform basis and made available to all teachers, including those in remote areas; secondly, it should be provided systematically, with a meaningful sequence built into the provision rather than a set of haphazard choices, however rich they may be; thirdly, it should offer a clear advantage to each teacher concerned, as well as to his or her school and to the educational service as a whole.

It would be a step in the right direction if teachers were encouraged to regard in-service education as both a professional right and a duty. Indeed, serious consideration should be given to including the entitlement to it in all teachers' contracts. Serious consideration should also be given to the proposal that an initial training qualification should have a specified maximum duration after which it should expire unless renewed by a minimum number of in-service courses taken and passed. In addition, much more attention needs to be paid to the provision of advanced qualifications conferring benefits in terms of salary and promotion.

Considerable emphasis has been given in recent years to the need for in-service teacher education to be school-based. At least two major reasons are advanced for this: cost-effectiveness and the benefits to the school and to teams of teachers of sharing in the mutual process of learning geared to the institutions' special aims. It would, however, be a mistake to regard the location of in-service education as a matter of choice of one or the other: for some teachers, the distance from day-to-day school affairs that external courses provide is a very valuable part of professional stimulus and reward. Where it is provided by an outside agency, part of the process of making the provision more systematic would be to encourage universities and other providers to organise their courses on a modular basis, so that individual credits could be accumulated sequentially so as to count towards a recognised advanced qualification such as a diploma or masters degree.

Professional development and improved career structures

It has been suggested[13] that one of the characteristics of the teaching profession is that it is more concerned with recruitment than with retention. Some able teachers certainly leave the profession after very few years of service never to return. Recently, however, wastage rates, in general, have tended to decline, despite frequently expressed fears that teachers are leaving the profession at an alarming rate. No doubt some teachers who would like to leave are put off by the lack of alternatives in the labour market[14].

Countries may wish to give more consideration to the need to make the teaching profession more attractive as a lifelong vocation by building in a more progressive career structure, closely associated with the kind of professional development recommended above as desirable in-service education. Good sequential programmes of in-service education not only improve the quality of teaching, but also make it possible for competent teachers to advance within their profession in a visible and rational manner. Possibly conflicting aims are to be seen in current policy pronouncements. In favour of making teaching an attractive lifelong career is recognition of the facts that it is a "craft" that takes many years to learn, that good classroom teachers should be encouraged to stay rather than be promoted into administration, and the growing fears of major shortages in the future. Against these can be set the aims of the creation of a teaching force with a broader range of occupational experience than at present by encouraging greater flows in and out of the profession.

In most countries, there are incremental scales for teachers' salaries, so that teachers earn more as they grow older irrespective of the quality of their teaching or additional qualifications achieved (though the length of time it takes to reach the maximum salaries varies widely; European data show Italy to be a country where the optimum is reached at a relatively late age while the United Kingdom is at the other extreme[15]). This is inevitable to some extent, but the automatic incremental increases should be accompanied by other means of gaining promotion or other salary-related recognition. Competent teaching should be rewarded, although it is notoriously difficult to achieve methods of teacher assessment or appraisal which are both fair and acceptable to the profession (see Chapter 7). Nevertheless, some countries have made more progress in this respect than others, and a good deal of benefit can be obtained from careful comparative studies. In any case, the appraisal of teaching quality should be regarded as part of a process of professional development rather than as a way of disciplining teachers. If appraisal is seen positively as an aspect of staff development rather than negatively as a means of sanctioning or dismissing the incompetent, then the whole process of professional development is much more likely to be both effective and acceptable[16].

In those countries where teacher appraisal is effective as part of professional development, it tends to be a well organised systematic process of reporting, often on an annual basis. Inevitably, there are dangers of such reports becoming bureaucratic and impersonal, but there is no need for this to be so. However, to introduce teacher appraisal without adequate in-service education and without an acceptable career structure is likely to be very unproductive.

To be able to judge teacher effectiveness is essential for education authorities but it has to be recognised that all methods of teacher appraisal are controversial and problematic. It must be emphasized that the quality of teaching performance cannot be measured by pupil achievement alone. Student outcomes are important, but the achievement of a pupil in reading, for example, depends not on one teacher but on several, as well as on many external factors. Moreover, there are different routes towards the same good results, rather than "one-best" model of good teaching. Student outcomes should be regarded as the responsibility of individual teachers, of departments, and of the whole school — not the responsibility of one teacher. This is one of many difficulties of teacher appraisal. Another difficulty is how to achieve effective and fair methods of assessing teacher quality without consuming too much time and incurring costs greater than any benefits achieved.

THE CHANGING ROLE OF TEACHERS: MORALE AND MOTIVATION

In order to improve the quality of teaching in some countries it will be necessary to specify more clearly what is expected of teachers in their various schools. In recent years the role of the teacher has been changing, and the number of tasks to be undertaken has increased. There has been a tendency since the Second World War for teachers to take on welfare and health responsibilities as well as liaison with parents and other members of the local community. In addition, teachers now tend to be expected to have a concern for the all-round development of their pupils — emotional, physical and social, as well as purely academic, though this varies from country to country as recent comparative research has shown. At the same time, the difficulties facing teachers have increased: for some, heavy teaching loads or large classes, a diversity of student populations and needs, inadequacy of support personnel to facilitate classroom teaching, and the paucity of teaching materials, even those considered to be essential. Many schools are seen to be uncongenial environments for both teachers and students. Schools are sometimes under-resourced and buildings deteriorating. It is common for teachers to complain that they do not have adequate professional or sub-professional assistance to teach the major part of a class with a degree of success, or to give sufficient attention to under-achieving students. In these conditions can we then expect good results? Is it not a question of societies getting the schools and teachers that they deserve?

One expert on teacher education has commented:

"The way in which a society defines the role of its teachers is central to the design and implementation of teacher education programmes. In open, pluralistic multi-party states there is no single agreed role definition. Religious, political, industrial and commercial, social and educational power groups try in various ways to influence such definitions, usually identifying their own prescriptions with the public interest".[17]

It is thus very important for policy-makers to be clear about the role specification of their teachers and to adjust the provision of in-service education accordingly, as well as making appropriate arrangements for the career structure to reflect any changes in the role of the teacher. There is no one formula which will apply to that role in all countries; different historical and traditional factors will be very important, but it is essential for planners to specify what they expect the role of the teacher to be.

Teachers must certainly be prepared to modify their teaching styles in the light of changing demands. Despite the existence of the research findings reported in Chapter 1 which show that teachers tend to talk too much and expect their students to listen for far too long, the monologue is still the dominant teaching style in many countries. Question and answer routines also tend to be regarded as "real teaching", though this recitation pattern is also known to be notoriously ineffective. Further research is needed on how to implement reforms in teaching styles given this resistance to change. There are some obvious organisational constraints such as time and space; the choice of textbooks is also a major factor. Teachers have often been expected to take on curriculum planning roles without being given the opportunity to acquire the requisite competence. The need to match changes in the teaching process with adequate planning of in-service education and training emerges as a necessary principle.

More experimentation is required with alternative teaching strategies. Very often teachers' expectations are too low, especially of ethnic minority children or slow learners. Teaching quality is more likely to be associated with a "problem-solving pedagogy" rather than the kind of rigid curriculum which is centrally prescribed and associated with traditional teaching methods. What needs to be avoided is making the success of alternative strategies depend on the exhausting efforts of "super-teachers", rather than embedding in the organisational practice of the whole school. Such teachers are candidates for burnout and represent individual beacons rather than models of good general practice[18].

Some educationists speak of the ideal of every teacher being a "researcher". When clarified, this concept indicates the kind of teacher who reflects on his or her own teaching performance in such a way as to seek improved methods of solving classroom problems. In other words, the teacher as researcher is a professional who engages in experimenting, collecting data, recording results and evaluating his or her own achievements. The ideal is not remotely attainable, of course, if teachers are overloaded with duties and under constant stress.

CONCLUSIONS

Teaching tends not to attract enough of the most intellectually able young people into the profession. In recognising this fact, policy-makers have a number of possible options open to them. They can provide better salaries and better conditions of service; they can increase the size of the overall post-secondary education population thus increasing the size of the educated pool from which teachers are selected; they can increase the status of the profession in other ways. All these solutions are costly.

Of those recruited into the profession, some are not suited to teaching for personality reasons. The solution to this problem is of two kinds: first, the development of more effective selection procedures, possibly by involving practising teachers and by assessing candidates on pre-course teaching experience. More experimental evidence should be sought. The second kind of solution relates to identifying unsuccessful teachers in the classroom, giving them whatever help is possible including in-service education and further training, but if all else fails, encouraging them to leave the profession. It is important, however, to see teacher appraisal in the overall context of staff development.

Initial courses of teacher education tend to be regarded as of low academic status and insufficiently relevant to the world of the classroom. In some countries, policy-makers are trying to make better use of practising teachers by various "partnership" models; another solution may be to encourage research into curriculum development for teacher education which might result in national criteria for teacher education courses. Some interesting new views of educational theory are emerging which will provide a better basis for initial courses of training.

Of those successful teachers recruited into the profession, some decide not to remain. The reasons include the following: the quality of life within schools, low morale, poor prospects of promotion at a time of declining rolls, and lack of professional development and in-service education. None of these difficulties is insuperable. The quality of life in a school can be improved by school-based self-evaluation techniques accompanied by externally provided in-service courses on educational management and school organisation; the morale of teachers can be raised by improving conditions of service, and where necessary, salary levels; teachers are more likely to accept poor promotion prospects if other ways are found of providing professional satisfaction by means of a combination of professional development within an improved career structure. It is a two-way process. Teachers require unstinting public support and well-defined rights. In return, they must fully recognise their responsibilities and duties.

NOTES AND REFERENCES

1. OECD (1983), *Compulsory Schooling in a Changing World*, Paris, pp. 139-40.
2. OECD (1985), "OECD Ministers Discuss Education in Modern Society", Paris (document for general distribution), p. 46.
3. Coombs, P.H. (1985), *The World Crisis in Education*, Oxford University Press, Oxford.
4. See Wilson, J.D., Thomson, G.O.B., Millward, B., Keenan, T. (eds.) (1989), *Assessment for Teacher Development: Proceedings of an International Seminar*, Edinburgh, Scotland, June 1987, Falmer Press, London.
5. Rhoades, G. (1985), *The Costs of Academic Excellence in Teacher Education*, Graduate School of Education, University of California, Los Angeles.
6. Tuxworth, E.N. (1982), *Competency in Teaching*, Further Education Unit, London.
7. Taylor, W. (1965), "The University Teacher of Education in England", *Comparative Education*, Vol. 1, No. 3, pp. 193-201.
8. Department of Education and Science (1972), *Teacher Education and Training* (The James Committee), HMSO, London.
9. Taylor, J.K. and Dale, I.R. (1971), *A Survey of Teachers in Their First Year of Service*, University of Bristol School of Education, Bristol.

10. OECD (1971), *Training, Recruitment and Utilisation of Teachers in Primary and Secondary Education*, Paris.
11. OECD/CERI (1982), *In-Service Education and Training of Teachers: A Condition for Educational Change*, Paris.
12. Neave, G. (1987), "Challenges Met: Trends in Teacher Education 1975-1985", Introduction to *New Challenges for Teachers and their Education: National Reports on Teacher Education*, Standing Conference of European Ministers of Education, Strasbourg.
13. Lortie, D. (1975), *School Teacher: A Sociological Study*, University of Chicago Press, Chicago.
14. Schlechty, P. and Vance, V. (1981), "Do academically able teachers leave education?" *Phi Delta Kappan* Vol. 63, No. 2, pp. 106-112.
15. Commission of the European Communities (1988), *The Conditions of Employment of Teachers in the European Community*. Report of a study carried out for the Commission of European Countries and the Netherlands Ministry of Education and Science by the Stichting Research voor Beleid, Leiden, Luxembourg. Appendix 1.
16. A recent discussion of the issues of teacher appraisal is contained in Wilson, J.D. (1988), *Appraising Teaching Quality*, Hodder and Stoughton, London, Sydney, Auckland, Toronto.
17. Taylor, W. (1980), "Decisions for Teacher Educators", *Prospects*, Vol. X, No. 2.
18. This has been demonstrated concerning teachers involved in particular strategies, for example, the mainstreaming of handicapped pupils, where "super-teacher burnout" has been identified as a problem. See Biklen, D.P. (1985), "Mainstreaming: From Compliance to Quality", *Journal of Learning Disabilities*, Vol. 18, pp. 58-61.

Chapter 6

SCHOOL ORGANISATION

INTRODUCTION

One can look at schooling from a variety of viewpoints and by using a number of frameworks but many of the same elements keep recurring. In turning now to school organisation we are aware, therefore, that there will be overlaps with preceding chapters, particularly with that concerned with curriculum planning since organisational factors merit discussion only in so far as they can facilitate or hinder the pursuit of agreed curricular objectives. Forms of organisation, whether externally or internally imposed, are means and not ends, though they are frequently treated in that way.

It is not the business of this report to pass judgement on the specific models of school organisation adopted by countries or autonomous local authorities for that would be to encroach on their inalienable prerogatives. Thus, whether secondary schools are selectively or non-selectively organised depends upon political or ideological choice or a particular interpretation of evidence from educational research. The salient truth is that whatever the school models adopted by education authorities, most of the same needs and problems arise. In this section we shall be concerned, therefore, with those organisational factors that can affect the quality of the service offered in virtually all school systems.

Six factors are especially important:
- Cycles of schooling and articulation between levels;
- Size and pupil/teacher ratios;
- Time spent on task;
- Length of school day and year;
- Leadership and management structures and styles;
- The use of information technologies in schools and classrooms.

It can readily be seen that certain of these factors are largely controlled by education authorities rather than schools themselves. In other words, they can be manipulated if there is a will to do so and if the appropriate financial resources are made available. To discuss them may appear to be stating the obvious. But many customs and practices are so deeply entrenched as to go unquestioned even though they fly in the face of compelling arguments that they should be abandoned or greatly modified and for this reason need alternatives to be discussed. This chapter will conclude with a discussion of the use and potential of information technologies (ITs) in schools and classrooms, a topic that is at once about the organisation of learning, the curriculum, and teaching — the topics of the previous chapters of this part of the report.

CYCLES OF SCHOOLING AND ARTICULATION BETWEEN LEVELS

An outstanding question is how best to cluster the years of schooling. Does it make any difference whether pupils spend 4 or 5 or 6 years in the primary school and a correspondingly shorter or longer time in the lower secondary school? Does it make a difference whether pupils attend an all-through compulsory school or a primary followed by a lower secondary school? Is there any advantage in creating middle schools for the age group 10-14? How should the span of years be divided between lower and upper secondary education? If some authorities have looked systematically into the advantages and disadvantages of clustering school years in alternative cycles, the majority have taken the existing sequences as a *fait accompli*. Yet there do appear to be potential benefits from experimenting with alternative sequences.

One particular sequence — the all-through compulsory school — appears to have particular advantages, especially when, as in Denmark, teachers are all trained to teach at the lower secondary level as well as for primary education. In that country the same teacher may serve as the class teacher for an age cohort passing through the whole compulsory period of eight years, thereby getting to know thoroughly individual pupils and their parents. The sharp break at the transition from primary to lower secondary is thus avoided. The school can function without being overshadowed by the anticipatory demands of secondary education. Not least, teachers can be used in a versatile way to take classes at any level instead of being tied to a specific level.

There are also arguments in favour of adopting a middle school cycle for 10 or 11 to 14 year-olds. Since the needs of this age group are particular they call for particular treatment. The primary-to-secondary transition can be facilitated by sensitive curriculum planning and the judicious deployment of teachers. In practice, an all-through compulsory school can design the curriculum in three blocks — 1-3 or 4: 4 or 5-7 (middle school): 8-9 or 10.

However the period of schooling may be organised in cycles, there can be no dispute over the paramount need for continuity from one year or module of learning to the next. Yet historically, there have been sharp disjunctures and in many systems these still remain. Recently, however, the linking or articulating of levels has become a major priority for a number of education authorities. The reasons for insisting upon continuity ought to be obvious. Even bright pupils are likely to be disturbed when there is a sudden change of curriculum and pace of learning or transference from a familiar to an unfamiliar environment. How much more disturbing are brusque transitions for low-achieving students. The most notorious of breaks, namely that from primary to secondary, is so shattering for many pupils that they never recover from it. All children and young people need to feel themselves in a *secure* as well as stimulating environment.

Various measures can be adopted to ensure continuity. First, the curriculum can be so designed as to build links or bridges between one level and the next. Secondly, class teachers can accompany the same pupils through two or more years of the educational cycle. Thirdly, there can be regular contacts and coordinated curriculum planning between those teaching at the different levels. Fourthly, detailed records of students can be kept charting their progress from one year to another and giving each new teacher an accurate picture of their strengths and weaknesses. Care must be taken, of course, to ensure that teacher/pupil conflicts, not always to be blamed on the pupil, should not be passed on to the next stage in a pupil's career.

The major difficulty arises when a change of school coincides with a student's arrival at a new level as from primary to lower secondary or from lower secondary to upper secondary.

Close liaison between the school leaders and teachers in the two schools concerned is here essential. This can be arranged through regular meetings and exchange visits. Such liaison is essential between a lower secondary school and the primary schools that feed it and between upper secondary schools, however organised, and the lower secondary schools that feed them. The records of each student passing through each level must be passed over to the teachers who will assume responsibility for them at the next level.

SIZE AND PUPIL/TEACHER RATIOS

School size is a significant factor in determining the teaching and learning environment. Studies have tended to show that small schools have the advantage of creating a friendly atmosphere and a sense of community whereas large schools offer wider subject choices and opportunities for extra-curricular activities. It is important to attempt to combine both by various forms of internal organisation and the sharing of facilities, wherever possible, among smaller schools.

Even more significant is the question of school climate or ethos. Studies have shown staff commitment and active co-operation within schools to be very significant factors in distinguishing good schools from less effective ones. A balance between discipline and order on the one hand and a relaxed student population on the other is evidently desirable. All schools need to have clear goals or purposes which are accepted and understood by teachers, students and their parents. The support of extra-school agencies is also helpful.

The size of a class, on the face of it, is a crucial determinant of learning gains, common sense appearing to indicate that the smaller the class the higher the individual achievement[1]. Certainly, the methods used by the teacher are affected by the number of students to be taught. Thus, a small class facilitates individualised instruction. In terms of cognitive achievement as measured by success in examinations, however, research evidence shows that it takes a large reduction in class size to bring about a significant improvement in achievement. Postlethwaite[2] reports that in many OECD countries, the general finding is that between class sizes of 15 and 40 pupils, little differences of achievement can be perceived even though IEA studies produce examples where countries with very large class sizes out-perform those where the figure is between 20 and 30. That being so, it has to be considered whether a deliberate trade-off should be made between class size and other factors, notably the number of contact hours per teacher. In Japan, for instance, the average class size is significantly higher than in many of the other OECD countries but teachers are allowed more time for lesson preparation. Maintaining an existing class size may also make it possible for a school to employ, for example, more remedial teachers or teachers of special subjects such as music. In short, excessive class size is a barrier to effective teaching and, wherever possible, classes should be small enough to permit the teacher to give attention to each student. However, in some circumstances it may be more beneficial to devote additional resources to other purposes than reducing class size.

Another key factor concerns teaching loads and contact hours. There are significant differences between countries in the number of hours teachers are with a class in a week, and the number of students a teacher comes into contact with during a single week or a day. In the United States it is not uncommon for a secondary teacher to have a load of 130 students in a single day, which presents problems of marking and establishing adequate personal relations.

It has been suggested that the teaching load should be reduced to no more than 80 students. What is important in each school is not to take the existing teaching load for granted but to ascertain whether or not it is facilitating the learning process. As for education authorities, they should ask such questions as: Would teachers be more effective if they were required to teach fewer hours? Would teachers be more effective if they had to deal with fewer pupils? Choices will really be determined, of course, by the amount of financial resources available. What is unacceptable is to ignore or dismiss evidence showing that class sizes and teaching loads are adversely affecting teacher and pupil performance.

TIME ON TASK

The time factor

It is evident that the amount of time students spend in school is only significant for learning outcomes if that time is constructively used. Thus, it is perfectly possible for a group of pupils in a school offering 1 000 hours of class teaching a year to learn as much or more as a group in one offering 1 200 hours. What counts is whether all the time available is used actively or not. What also counts is the subject matter and balance of the curriculum. Thus, an education authority may have the best of intentions for its schools but prescribe a curriculum so broad that the pupils fail to master basic knowledge and skills.

Until recently, surprisingly little was known about how children really spend their time in school. That lack is being increasingly rectified and there has now been a good deal of research into the phenomenon, especially in the United States. Simultaneously, more and more education authorities are insisting that, without increasing, though perhaps redistributing, resources, schools should be more effective, for example in reducing rates of underachievement or drop-out. The onus is upon schools, therefore, to use the time of each pupil to the best possible advantage.

There is evidence, however, to show that many pupils are actively learning for only a part of the school day. Karweit states that:

> "(research studies) support the assertion that traditional schooling practices involve the child for only a small fraction of the school day. In many classrooms, much of the instructional time may be consumed with interruptions, distractions, discipline and other non-instructional activities."[3]

And Walker[4] has argued for the importance of time actually allocated to instruction as a factor in achievement.

One impediment to the optimal use of time in school may be the disruptive behaviour of individual pupils or groups of pupils. "While the focus varies — bullying and vandalism in France and Switzerland, bullying in Norway and Finland, truancy in Denmark, violence to teachers and pupils in the United Kingdom — there is consensus among educationalists that disruption is a problem"[5]. Thus, it is essential to identify students with disruptive habits at an early age and to ascertain what is bothering them and how they can be helped to fit in with their classmates. The fault may lie with the school or the teacher or misplaced pedagogy — a teacher's perception of disruption may be a student's perception of justifiable protest. The help of parents may be necessary. Consistently disruptive students may have to be suspended from school.

Another impediment to effective learning can be exceptional rates of absenteeism on the part of individual teachers or groups of teachers. This can lead to pupils losing a large amount of teaching time or being taught in merged classes where individualised attention is minimal or non-existent. Within each school the school leader or leaders must accordingly keep a close watch on teacher absenteeism to ensure that no particular class or group of pupils is penalised by the phenomenon. As for education authorities, they must monitor teacher attendance across the schools under their jurisdiction and take vigorous action whenever unacceptable absenteeism becomes noticeable in a given school.

Timing of the school day

The fact that the timing of the school day varies from country to country was perceived until recently as a factor of no special significance. Children may well learn better in the morning than in the afternoon. If this is so, it would plead in favour of an early start to the school day and ending it at about 13.00 or 13.30, which is, of course, the traditional pattern in some countries such as Germany. Other arguments may be added in favour of this arrangement. For instance, afternoons could be used for practical studies in laboratories and workshops, for doing homework and taking part in extra-curricular activities, including sport. Teachers could use afternoons for preparation of classes, marking and meetings. Moreover, if the claim is justified that higher quality should be attained by redeploying resources, then there are economies to be made in maintaining morning as against all-day schools.

There are counter-arguments, of course, that mainly have to do with family and other social priorities. For example, who will look after children with both parents working? Who is going to supervise their homework? We would only point out that there is room for systematic research into the relationship between the distribution of time during the school day and learning outcomes. At least, there should be an honest appraisal of whether schools are being used all the time as places of learning or only part of the time. This should include appraisals of experiments with flexible timetabling such as the *temps mobile* in some French *collèges* and *lycées* which nevertheless adhere to the same total number of hours worked by teachers, by pupils, and in each subject[6]. Mobility and flexibility in the organisation of time are founded on the principle of the annual time-budget which functions in practice through the setting up of teams of teachers from different subjects who teach in units of three or four classes.

The uses of homework

"Although on balance the findings support the view that homework contributes to school achievement, the designs have often inhibited any likelihood of demonstrating such a relationship. There is a need to disentangle the homework issue from emotional argument and to see it in its true perspective; as an aspect of overall time on task which, by the end of secondary school, apparently contributes as much to achievement in some subjects as the time allocated during regular school hours."[7]

"The 15 empirical studies of homework that have been conducted since 1900 showed that the assignment and grading of work done at home produces an effect on achievement that is three times as large as family socio-economic status (as indexed by parental income, education and occupation)."[8]

These two representative quotations are cited to show that the popular impression about the academic value of homework appears to be reinforced by empirical evidence. The academic factor must be stressed because there are objections to the use of homework on the grounds that it restricts the non-academic lives of children and that it is socially discriminatory seeing that children from overcrowded or culturally-deprived homes cannot study as favourably at home as their more privileged peers, or find such study impossible.

The response to the first objection is that homework does not have to be so excessive as to encroach on the child's extra-curricular activities. The response to the second is not to abolish homework, because children from more "educated" homes are still likely to receive parental support for out-of-school study, even to the point of being sent for private tuition: cramming schools are flourishing in more than one OECD country with the *jukku* in Japan as perhaps the most widely-known example. The response is rather to find ways and means of helping deprived children to study outside regular school hours. Where possible, this might involve doing homework in school at the end of the school day. It might also mean the use of public libraries and other public facilities out of school hours. Teachers can also strive as far as possible to give pupils all the necessary reading and other materials required to complete a homework assignment.

THE SCHOOL DAY AND YEAR

Length of school day and year

Experience shows that it is unconscionably difficult to change the existing pattern of the school day and year in any given country, not least because of powerful economic and social interests that depend on the *status quo*. Yet, undoubtedly some patterns are more desirable than others[9]. A central question is how important is the sheer quantity of time spent in school and in related school studies. For that quantity varies to a surprising degree from country to country as well as between regions and between school districts within certain countries. The two controlling factors are the number of days spent in school in one year and the length of the school day.

In virtually all countries, the number of days spent annually in school has increased considerably over the past century. In recent times, the length of compulsory schooling has been prolonged and an increasing percentage of young people, up to virtually 100 per cent in a few countries, have stayed in secondary education up to the end of the cycle. At the same time, pre-school attendance has experienced a dramatic expansion. All this means that human beings spend a large slice of their lives in school. More importantly, it means that differences between countries and between regions within countries in the amount of time spent in school annually add up to very striking disparities for the compulsory cycle, even more so for completion of the secondary cycle. Thus, in a country with an annual attendance rate of 1 000 hours per pupil we arrive at a total of 9 000 hours for completing the compulsory cycle and 12 000 hours for completing 12 years. By contrast, in a country with an annual attendance rate of 1 200 hours we arrive at a total of 10 800 hours for completing the compulsory cycle and 14 400 hours for completing the whole cycle. That yields overall differences of 1 800 hours and 2 400 hours, respectively. Assuming that the time is used equally constructively in both countries, and that longer is therefore better, it can be seen that the latter enjoys a substantial advantage over the former. Individual countries and independent local education authorities may find it salutary to compare their aggregate attendance requirements for each pupil with requirements in other countries and independent local authorities. The findings of the IEA on this phenomenon can readily be consulted. Needless to say, any decision to lengthen the school year has far-reaching financial implications, mainly in that it entails an increase in salaries of teachers and other staff.

Absenteeism

Of course, as pointed out above, the length of the school day and year is only significant if pupils take full advantage of the time available. What happens, however, to pupils who for one reason or another are frequently absent from school? Attendance at the primary school level is regular almost everywhere but in some countries more or less serious absenteeism consistently occurs at the lower secondary level within the compulsory period. Such absenteeism is greater in urban than in suburban areas and related to age, sex, race, school performance, and, not least, the difficulty of applying sanctions against absence. In some schools and school districts absenteeism may attain such a level as to become a blight that it is convenient to ignore.

All schools are likely to have at least some pupils who are absent more than the average and the continuity of whose learning is disrupted. This problem is usually solved by the efficient use of class teachers charged with the task of noting and following up all cases of exceptional absenteeism and, where appropriate, involving the assistance of trained specialists to deal with it. Given the lack of strong sanctions, it is the support and co-operation of parents that, in the last resort, is the critical factor.

Far more critical is the case of schools where absenteeism affects many pupils and is endemic. Then the question arises: where does the blame lie? Is it not, above all, the fault of the school or the school system? Perhaps school resources are inadequate. If so, who is to be responsible for dealing with the problem? Can the solution be left to the school itself or is it necessary to apply external sanctions against offending schools or school systems?

Rhythm of the school year

It is well known that the distribution of time over the school year — mainly the number, length and occurrence of terms — was fixed in most countries during the nineteenth century, under quite different working and social conditions from today, and has stood firm despite attempts in some countries to change it. The long summer break still largely prevails in spite of evidence that students, especially low-achieving ones, lose a little or a critical amount of the learning gained during the previous academic year. Research and common sense thus combine to advocate shorter terms and more frequent and shorter breaks. As for the school day, there is powerful social opposition to changing the rhythm of the school year. Perhaps, the answer is to seek to bring about change over an extended period by means of gradual increments.

One option is the four-term year in contrast with the three-term or two-semester year whereby the school terms are shorter and are of approximately equal length with a less dominant long vacation. This is under discussion in the United Kingdom, though with no government plans for change in this direction, and in New Zealand; it is already in operation in most of Australia and parts of the United States. The advantage claimed for this arrangement is educational — shorter terms allowing for more concentrated study and lower levels of stress, including teacher stress. Research has yet to prove, however, that shorter terms do lead to better performance[10].

LEADERSHIP AND MANAGEMENT: STRUCTURES AND STYLES

There is in OECD countries an increasing consensus that positive school leadership is a necessary prerequisite of effective schooling. Thus, OECD Ministers of Education, meeting in 1984, emphasized in their final communiqué the importance of "qualitative factors affecting the performance of schools, including school-based leadership"[11]. But there is no consensus about the ways in which leadership should be organised and exercised. The most striking dissension is over the role of principals or heads (hereafter termed principals). If the education authorities in some countries believe in the need for a strong principal with wide pedagogical and managerial powers, others are wedded to the practice of collegial direction and management, and others again rely on a significant measure of external managerial control through school boards or inspectors or strictly enforced rules and regulations.

A second issue concerns how far school leadership and management should be internal to the school. What is the case for a greater or lesser measure of external engagement in the running of schools? These two issues will be discussed in this section.

The powerful principal

Support for the idea of the powerful principal comes from a number of recent reports and research studies in certain OECD countries. In the United Kingdom, for example, a report by HMI on ten secondary schools found that the most important single factor in these schools' success was the quality of leadership of the principal[12]. In a report on a school-based teacher training project in England, Baker[13] highlighted the positive contribution that principals can make to innovation. He concluded that the commitment of the principal and senior management teams appeared to have been decisive for the successful implementation of the project. His diagnosis has been echoed in studies on staff development by the Rand Corporation in the United States; principals, it is said, play an active role because it is they who must influence teachers' responses to school improvement initiatives[14]. It was for that reason that Goodlad[15], in his description of the genesis of the League of Cooperating Schools Project, stated that the role of the principal was strategic as much in impeding as in facilitating change. Fullan[16], in his review of American and Canadian research, also concluded that the positive or negative role of the principal has a critical influence on teachers' receptiveness to new ideas. Robinson[17] argues that the New Zealand approach to school self-appraisal has erred in allocating a relatively neutral role to the principal and believes that the principal's role is critical in ensuring the effective implementation of any appraisal.

In an analysis of surveys covering France, Germany, Sweden and the United Kingdom, McHugh and Parkes[18] noted that, despite the obvious differences in the education systems described, the concepts, issues, and problems concerned were very similar. Esp[19] came to much the same conclusion in his survey of leadership training in Denmark, France, the Netherlands, Norway, and Sweden, although he further stated that training programmes naturally reflected the educational, professional, political, cultural, and geographical features of each country reviewed. These included the breakdown of responsibilities between school principals and school managers, on the one hand, and leaders at the various education authority levels (superintendents, inspectors or local education authority directors, the central inspectorate and so on), on the other.

The powers of principals are often very considerable. In the United Kingdom, for example, they are recognised as playing a key role in developing the curriculum, devising assessment policies, managing the teaching staff and identifying their in-service needs, fostering good relationships with the surrounding communities, and giving the individual school its particular "ethos". In the United States, principals are expected to play a key role in fostering school and community support for needed reforms, and are sometimes freed from the burdens of administration and maintaining discipline in order to concentrate on curriculum renewal. In European countries with a tradition of centralised control, principals are expected to play a part in promoting teaching. The recent development of various school-based appraisal procedures[20] designed to result in school projects capable of solving major problems in such traditionally centralised countries as Belgium, France, the Netherlands, and Sweden, constitutes a means of involving principals and their deputies directly in the implementation of measures to improve the quality of schooling. It follows from these differences that the applicability of national research findings concerning effective principals to other countries depends critically on the educational, political, and cultural traditions in place. A strong principal may be highly effective in a system that calls for clear leadership if decisions are to be taken at all. It does not follow that this authoritative figure is a *sine qua non* of effective management where this does not obtain.

Participatory decision-making and management

There exist three models for organising school leadership embracing, or as alternatives to, the powerful principal model:

— a pyramidal hierarchy;
— collegial leadership;
— the teaching staff or the whole staff electing a *primus inter pares* for a fixed term.

In Denmark, there are school principals but the collegial approach prevails in practice. In Portugal, the second model is in use; in Spain, the third. What is striking, however, is that in the countries where the powerful principal idea prevails, the apparently contradictory idea of participatory decision-making is simultaneously gaining ground.

Clearly, the responsibility for certain important decisions cannot be left to the discretion of one individual. Greater responsibility and autonomy at local level must be coupled with genuine participation by all concerned: teachers, parents, and pupils from beyond a certain age, with a view to developing a spirit of collective endeavour. That concern for participation reflects also the tendency to decentralise powers and responsibilities in countries that historically have had centralised administrative systems. Opening up schools to the community implies engaging in a dialogue with the various interest groups concerned. Thus, the national reports on strengthening education systems in the United States stress that the task of revitalising education is one that belongs not just to the schools but to everyone working in concert — parents, community leaders, business people, students themselves, as well as educators. Participatory machinery has been introduced not only in schools but in the local and regional administrative hierarchy as well.

The wider context of management

However great the autonomy enjoyed by schools, they are still answerable to administrative authorities at local, regional and national level that have responsibility for:

— Setting quality targets and providing the means of attaining them;
— Monitoring the implementation of appropriate strategies;
— Conducting regular appraisals of performance in association with the schools concerned.

In other words, the creation of a better climate for learning does not depend solely on a school's own intellectual and material resources or its own efforts through self-appraisal to produce relevant curriculum and programmes. The public authorities at their different levels must sustain such efforts in line with national and regional objectives. Moreover, where schools show little initiative, it may be necessary to push them in desired directions from outside. A recent United States guide[21], for example, enjoins superintendents to develop those school leadership capacities required by proposed reforms and to support and monitor improvements.

Support systems

In practice, it is not always easy to harmonize and integrate both internal and external school resources. Many local authorities charged with offering external support are not in fact equal to the task, either because they lack the ability to relate meaningfully to schools or because their attitudes are hierarchical or mistrustful with regard to school-based initiatives. In such instances, higher-level regional or national authorities, including the central inspectorate where one exists, may be called upon to intervene.

External support does not consist solely of technical assistance to the school to improve the quality of education on a continuing basis. The school environment may serve either to impede or foster efforts to identify and provide quality schooling. Structures and groups outside the school may exert a pull in a particular direction, depending on their influence in the local or regional decision-making process, particularly in a context of decentralisation and more collective decision-making. Parents' associations, teachers' unions or associations, community groups with an interest in education, local administrators can play a major role in sustaining a school's improvement efforts. However, it is essential that these interest groups do not seize the opportunity to push a particular interpretation of quality that is not favourable to other groups less able to press their interests. Should this occur, the school leadership may well be caught in a cross-current of complex socio-cultural influences and seek in vain for mediation which the technical and non-professional support structures would be unable to provide.

A problem often arises because of the ambiguous powers of external bodies that combine an advisory or consultative as well as a monitoring role, which is not always understood or accepted by some schools and some teachers. This occurs in countries where the inspectorate or the local/regional education authority is vested with both functions, although inspectorates have tended increasingly to assume a consultative function, with the responsible authorities delegating the inspectors' former advisory duties to pedagogical advisers[22].

A word must be said finally about possible divergences in how the various authorities with power to influence schools directly or indirectly perceive their interventionist and evaluation roles. Are clear directives always provided as to how quality in education is to be pursued? Do the authorities mandated to allocate resources to this end always have the means to put policies into practice? Are the support and evaluation systems available of sufficient worth and quantity? And in those countries that are pursuing policies to devolve powers to the school level, is sufficient attention being given to the support services required to enable schools to function effectively?

Selection and training of school leaders

It might appear gratuitous to insist that the criteria for recruiting principals and other school leaders should correspond to the profiles of the tasks required of them. In reality, however, these criteria are frequently not clear and explicit or else have scarcely evolved in recent years and "the authorities should focus all their attention on the selection of principals who occupy a key position in the effective running of the school. This is an important link in the supervisory chain"[23]. In response to this need, in the United Kingdom for instance, the Department of Education and Science sponsored a substantial research effort in this field[24] and the authorities are working out guidelines for the selection and appointment of school principals. There are plans for research as well as seminars in local authorities. In the United States, a number of reports have stressed that states should set vigorous standards for recruiting, training and monitoring the performance of principals. There is a series of interesting initiatives involving the National Association of Secondary School Principals (NASSP) that apply extensive job analysis and assessment centre techniques to the selection and training of principals[25].

A number of guidelines is gradually becoming available on new training standards for principals and school leaders. These seldom include a detailed evaluation of the results of such training. Several models currently coexist. For example, two countries with a tradition of centralisation, France and Sweden, have established highly-decentralised training schemes, with principals themselves playing a major part in training provision. But whereas in France the emphasis is on initial training, in Sweden it is on in-service training. In England and Wales, a special centre has been charged with the task of promoting the development of efficient training courses, *inter alia* through compiling comparative data. Many Member countries are now seeking ways of initiating principals and school leaders more systematically into their new duties.

The practical requirements of training for senior staff is raising a host of questions. Who are to be included? To what extent, for example, should primary school principals, secondary schools principals, deputy principals, local authority or school district advisers or administrators all receive the same or largely the same training? What part should employers, institutions of higher education, and the administration/teaching profession play? How long should the training be? What can theory and research contribute to the training and practice of educational leadership[26]?

INFORMATION TECHNOLOGIES IN SCHOOLS AND CLASSROOMS

The arrival of information technologies (ITs) in schools has been heralded by some as a potential revolution in long-entrenched habits and patterns in the organisation of learning, while others predict a valuable but more limited role. In fact, information technologies have already become an integral part of modern education systems. A CERI report categorised the different patterns that countries were pursuing in introducing ITs in schools as: the "vocational" approach (where ITs are introduced primarily as a response to the need for specialised manpower), the "comprehensive" approach (where informatics is regarded as part of general education for all), the "equipment" approach (priority given to investment in equipment as a variant of the "vocational" approach), and the "curriculum" approach (predominated by purely educational concerns, especially curriculum development for ITs)[27]. A more recent survey of the extent to which countries have introduced microcomputers in schools has refined the picture further — there are more microcomputers in secondary schools than in primary schools while the patterns of use at the two levels are often different. Microcomputers are mostly used at the primary level for teaching traditional subjects and basic skills. In the secondary schools, in many but not all countries, microcomputers have led primarily to the creation of new subjects such as computer awareness at junior levels, and computer science at senior secondary levels and in vocational schools[28].

That survey documented the extent to which microcomputers have become a reality in schools; in Austria, Australia, Denmark, France, Iceland, the Netherlands, the United Kingdom and the United States, it is claimed that all secondary schools now have an average of between 10 and 20 microcomputers. National data are not available for Canada and Switzerland, but figures supplied by certain provinces and cantons indicate that these countries are equally well equipped. Other countries with smaller stocks of equipment have indicated their intentions to increase the supply.

While the IT advocates enthusiastically predict major changes to teaching and learning, it should be underlined that the actual impact of the new technology is not simple or one-way. It depends very much on the choices education authorities and teachers make about how it should be used. The range of possible uses is broad. Microcomputers can provide the basis for the introduction of new subjects to the curriculum or for the development of new topics within existing subjects. As teaching tools, they can be used, mundanely, to replicate and perhaps reduce the drudgery of known teaching methods, such as drill and practice, or more radically, to structure learning based on exploration and discovery. They can also be used to support new approaches to the assessment and monitoring of student progress. Beyond this range of applications, new products are now available that lead to a questioning of existing pedagogical theories and introduce approaches to learning which could not be envisaged without computer technology[29].

How far new approaches are adopted will depend crucially in turn on the attitudes and capacities of teachers. They will need to be ready to learn new content and methods of classroom management. To the extent that microcomputers are used in applications more complex than simple drill and practice, they will need to become directly involved in applied research into what is taught and how it is learned. By extension, this implies that teachers should become partners in the development of curriculum and the specification of software. On this view, they would exercise a considerable degree of control over professional knowledge. To formalise and disseminate the knowledge that they develop, expert teachers may require release from their regular duties in order to work with teams which include professional programmers and teacher educators where teachers provide software specifications, and the programmers produce the disks.

To exploit ITs fully, teachers will need to draw upon other human and material resources continually and possibly in greater measure than has been typical in the past. Such resources include adequate professional development and INSET, appropriately-designed software, and access to computers. To provide access to one or two without sufficient access to all three may well prove ineffective. It is important to note that the problem is not necessarily one of sufficient resources, but instead of how to co-ordinate the resources already available. In this connection, new co-ordinating structures may need to be established to ensure that teachers are trained in sufficient numbers and on applications in line with the likely educational uses of microcomputers and the probable access to hardware and software within the school.

Whether quality is thereby enhanced can only be assessed on the basis of concrete experience. The mere introduction of ITs alone will not necessarily be beneficial, except in the minimal sense of providing familiarisation with the everyday tools of modern society, unless the software is itself of good quality[30] and its application in the curriculum imaginatively and coherently integrated into overall programmes to meet the learning needs of youngsters. But the potential for raising quality is clear and manifold — through the development of new curricula and styles of learning, through the professional stimulus it can provide to teachers, through the motivation it can give to youngsters, including both the high-flyers and those who otherwise would be counted among the school's low-achievers. For the latter, the new forms of self-directed learning opened up by ITs may often be more attractive than traditional methods. However, to generalise the benefits of ITs will require careful scrutiny of questions of organisation and cost if they are to give substance to some of the more enthusiastic claims of their advocates.

NOTES AND REFERENCES

1. Statistics on average class size and pupil/teacher ratios prove much harder to compile, and certainly to compare across countries, than is commonly supposed. Factors that render teacher/pupil ratios incomparable include varying definitions of what count as "teachers", and different methods of accommodating part-time teachers and whether they are included as "full-time equivalents". This topic is being analysed in current OECD work on the statistics of education and is intended to be included in a future edition in the series *Education in OECD Countries: Comparative Statistics*.

2. Postlethwaite, T.N. (1986), "Research on Quality with Special Emphasis on International Findings" (OECD working document).

3. Karweit, N. (1986), "The Organisation of Time in Schools: Time Scales and Learning", Philadelphia (unpublished).

4. Walker, D.A. (1976), *The IEA Six Subject Survey: An Empirical Study of Education in Twenty-One Countries*, John Wiley and Sons, New York.

5. Steed, D. (1985), "Disruptive Pupils, Disruptive Schools: Which is the Chicken? Which is the Egg?", *Educational Research*, Vol. 27, No. 1, February, p. 3.

6. Husti, A. (1985), "Temps Mobile", *Rencontres Pédagogiques, Recherches Pratiques*, Institut National de Recherche Pédagogique, No. 1. Paris. 126 pp.
7. Thomas, R.M. (1985), "The Use of Homework," in *International Encyclopaedia of Education*, Pergamon, Oxford, New York, Toronto, Sydney, Paris, Frankfurt. p. 2294.
8. Walberg, H.J. (1984), "Families as Partners in Educational Productivity", *Phi Delta Kappan*, Vol. 65, No. 6, p. 399.
9. OECD/PEB (1988), "Time for a Change?" (Conclusions of a Seminar on the Organisation of School Time and its Implications for Buildings, held in Ouranoupoli, Greece, 11-16 October, 1987), Paris (document for general distribution).
10. *Ibid.* p. 11.
11. OECD (1984), Meeting of the Education Committee at Ministerial Level: "Quality in Education" Communiqué, Press/A(84)64. See also Stegö, N.E., Gielen, K., Glatter, R., Hord, S.M. (eds.) (1987), *The Role of School Leaders in School Improvement*, OECD/CERI, published by ACCO, Leuven (Belgium).
12. Department of Education and Science (1977), *Ten Good Schools: A Secondary School Inquiry*, HMSO, London.
13. Baker, K. (1981), "The Site Project; Final Report" (mimeo), University of Bristol, School of Education.
14. Mann, D. (1976), "The Politics of Training Teachers in Schools", *Teachers' College Record*, Vol. 77, No. 3.
15. Goodlad, J. (1976), *Facing the Future*, McGraw Hill, London.
16. Fullan, M. (1981), "The Role of Human Agents Internal to School Districts in Knowledge Utilisation", in Lehming, R. and Kane, M. *Improving Schools: Using What We Know*, Sage Publications, Beverly Hills and London.
17. Robinson, V.M.J. (1982), "The Intermediate In-school Review: A Critical Evaluation of a Model for School Improvement" (mimeo), University of Auckland, Education Department.
18. McHugh, R. and Parkes, D. (1978), "Editorial", *Educational Administration*, Vol. 7, No. 1.
19. Esp, D. (1980), "Selection and Training of Secondary School Senior Staff: Some European Examples", *Education*, 17th October.
20. Hopkins, D. (1985), *School-Based Review for School Improvement: A Preliminary State-of-the-Art*, ACCO, Leuven.
21. Council for Educational Development and Research (1984), *A Response to the National Reports on School Reform — the Superintendent's Can-do Guide to School Improvement*, Washington D.C
22. OECD/CERI (1978), *Creativity of the School: Conclusions of a Programme of Enquiry*, Paris (in particular Chapter V: "The Role of the Inspectorate").
23. Statement by Mr. Daniel Coens, Education Minister, Belgium (Dutch-speaking sector) at the meeting of the Education Committee at Ministerial Level (1984).
24. The POST project, the main results of which are found in: Morgan, C., Hall, V., and MacKay, H. (1983), *The Selection of Secondary Headteachers*, Open University Press, Milton Keynes, and in Hall, V., MacKay, H., and Morgan, C. (1986), *Secondary School Headteachers*, Open University Press, Milton Keynes.
25. See, for example, Hersey, P. (1989), "Identifying and Developing Superior Principals", in Wilson, J.D., Thomson, G.O.B., Millward, B., Keenan, T. (forthcoming), *Assessment for Teacher Development: Proceedings of an International Seminar*, Edinburgh, Scotland, June 1987, Falmer Press, London.
26. Bolam R. (1983), "Strategies for School Improvement", OECD/CERI, Paris (document for general distribution).

27. OECD/CERI (1986), *New Information Technologies: A Challenge for Education*, Paris.
28. SED/OECD (1988), *Microcomputers and Secondary Teaching: Implications for Teacher Education* (Report on an International Seminar arranged by the Scottish Education Department in co-operation with OECD, 12-15 October, 1987), Glasgow; and OECD (1988), "The Use of Microcomputers in Education: Implications for Education" (OECD working document), Paris.
29. OECD/CERI (1987), *Information Technologies and Basic Learning: Reading, Writing, Science and Mathematics*, Paris.
30. See OECD/CERI (1989), *Information Technologies in Education: The Quest for Quality Software*, Paris.

Chapter 7

ASSESSMENT, APPRAISAL AND MONITORING

THE NEED FOR ASSESSMENT

In Chapter 4, we considered evaluation in relation to curriculum planning and design in schools. In this chapter, we are concerned more widely with pupil assessment, teacher appraisal, and the monitoring of school systems and whole education systems. Since the meanings of technical terms in this field are often confusing, the following distinctions have been suggested[1] for the sake of clarity:

— *Evaluation* is a general term used to describe any activity where the quality of provision is the subject of systematic study;
— *Appraisal* emphasizes the forming of qualitative judgements about an activity, a person, or an organisation;
— *Assessment* implies the use of measurement and/or grading based on known criteria.

Every school needs a system for evaluating pupils' learning, but methods vary from country to country and even from school to school. Each country also needs to have reliable and regular information about overall school and teacher performance. Both of these involve pupil assessment but differences exist in what use is made of such information. No school system can be regarded as satisfactory where no assessment takes place; regular appraisal of pupils' work is an essential part of the teaching and learning process. It is, however, quite possible to envisage efficient school systems where examinations as such do not exist, and the Swedish example is discussed below.

There has been a general tendency for teachers to be given more formal assessment responsibilities. In some schools and school systems, this has meant that assessment by teachers has become a significant aspect of the evaluation procedure even to the point of replacing public examinations.

In order to increase the quality of education by means of assessment procedures, it would seem evident that teachers need to develop expertise in the formative, diagnostic use of tests. In Sweden, for example, where school examinations have been abandoned, teachers have access to nationally-produced diagnostic testing material on an entirely voluntary basis — that is, they can prepare their own diagnostic materials if they prefer. At the school level, every institution is required to set up procedures to discuss the working arrangements for diagnostic testing and to remedy any shortcomings in the system. At regional level, school councils play a role in inspecting, servicing and development. In Sweden, the tradition of national evaluation is not strong, and until recently there was little enthusiasm for evaluating the whole system; much more attention has been paid to testing of a diagnostic kind at the level of the individual pupil. As in the Netherlands, however, this is now undergoing change and national assessment mechanisms are being developed.

In some countries, in contrast with Sweden, there is a strong tradition of using formal examinations as a means of assessment at individual pupil and school level where they are seen to have two main functions: the diagnosis of abilities and learning problems as well as a prognostic function to indicate future performance. One of the problems here is the comparability of examination results across school systems. In order to combat this difficulty, guidelines have been accepted by all the *Länder* in Germany, for example, on the reproduction and application of knowledge or skills, and problem-solving. This has been a useful and productive exercise. Criteria are supplied in this way but the ultimate responsibility lies with the professional judgement of individual teachers.

General support is being given in most countries to increased assessment at primary level, where it sometimes happens that there is neither a clearly outlined curriculum nor an adequate means of assessment, especially given the tendency to abolish formal examinations. In Switzerland, interesting experimental work is taking place which appears to have general applicability to the problem[2]. Research there and elsewhere has shown that the traditional evaluation of pupils' performance often fails to achieve its objectives. Commonly, it does not help the pupils to improve, it does not accurately inform parents of their child's progress, and it does not give sufficient information to educationists to enable them to plan the child's educational future. Difficulties arise partly because the main function of marking is not clear; there can be no single all-purpose mark that is simultaneously predictive, a credentialling device, and a diagnostic tool, but that is what teachers have tried to employ. In primary schools, the process of assessment is also sometimes distorted by marks being used to punish or reward. In addition, teachers find it difficult to transform a record of under-achievement into a prescription for remedying it.

The Swiss research indicates that while formal evaluation instruments and data banking have a role to play, the main solution lies elsewhere. Thus, in one experimental project, teachers were encouraged to prepare their own diagnostic tests, and marks were not given though mistakes were carefully analysed and explained to the pupil. Twice a year remarks, not grades, were entered in parents' notebooks giving an account of the child's progress. Each June an evaluation of the whole year was noted in the pupil's record. Teachers recorded the achievement made during the year but there was no comparison between pupils — in other words, the purpose of this evaluation was diagnostic not rank-ordering. Surveys showed that parents and teachers favoured the new evaluation despite the work load involved, but there was a clear need for teachers to receive more training with a view to encouraging them to discard their old ideas about marking, and to develop their skills in being more precise about objectives and in the construction of their own diagnostic materials. The great advantage of this evaluation project has been the emphasis on the professional expertise of the teachers and their need to communicate more effectively both with pupils and with their parents. At primary level, it has been considered appropriate to give the diagnostic function of evaluation priority over the other functions.

At secondary level, there is also general recognition of the need to strengthen the diagnostic function of assessment. Some countries further stress the need for improved examination techniques both as a means of helping individual pupils and their teachers but also as a useful comparative tool for national and international analyses. Although misgivings are evident about the possibility of over-examining and the perverse effects of examinations, countries are experimenting with the use of criterion-referencing and item banks for school examinations.

The use of item banks as a way of improving tests and examinations is under consideration in a number of countries. Possibilities of computerisation and computer access already exist. Related ideas include: profiles (*dossiers* in France), and records of achievement; mastery learning and testing; graded tests (with or without criterion-referencing); tailored tests. Some countries, such as France and Australia, are moving away from formal examinations towards greater use of continuous assessment; Sweden has already done so. In the United Kingdom, there is a policy of giving continuous assessment more importance as a complement to formal examinations.

School systems in most countries have tended in the past to be too much concerned with psychometric methods and too little concerned with educational measurement which deals with a student's achievement in its own right, which tests for competence rather than reflects intelligence, and which is not concerned with the "experimental controls" so typical of psychological measurement. Criterion-referencing is not the only answer, and not necessarily the best solution, to these problems. School-based assessment, with properly motivated and trained teachers, is regarded by some as offering a better long-term solution. Such a solution would be part of professional accountability, involving teacher expertise, whereas reliance on public examinations tends to be associated with market accountability involving consumer choice in a field where the basis of choice can be dubious.

As with many of the other policies and suggestions for improving quality considered in this part of the report, the success of new and complex methods of assessment depends upon a high level of skill and commitment on the part of teachers. Teaching traditional curricula using the old, well-tried methods of pupil assessment was a relatively simple matter: the teacher possessed certain knowledge (mostly factual information) which had to be absorbed and reproduced by pupils. The teacher's task was to present the information in manageable packages, the pupils memorised the information, and after an interval the teacher tested the pupils' recall. Correct and incorrect answers could be easily identified, and pupils given a corresponding mark. All of the above avenues of improving pupil learning using various evaluation and assessment techniques would clearly fall to the ground where such a limited approach is commonplace. Returning to the typology of conceptions of the teachers' tasks presented in Chapter 1 — teaching as labour, as craft, as a profession, or as an art — the teacher cannot be regarded and treated as a mere educational labourer. That must be fully reflected in any approaches taken to teacher appraisal.

THE APPRAISAL OF TEACHERS

Among suggestions for reform second only in prominence to assessing the progress of students is the question of the professional appraisal of teachers. In many countries, teachers are civil servants and possess similar job security to others with that status[3]. Nevertheless, it is seen as important that they shall be regarded as professionals, submitting their expertise to regular appraisal, and in extreme cases being transferred to non-teaching duties. In most OECD countries, teachers have security of tenure of some kind, but it is to be emphasized that the dismissal of incompetent teachers is not the major question in serious discussions about teacher appraisal, though certain education authorities now deliberately use appraisal procedures for identifying and removing teachers who fall below a minimum level of competence. In so far as there is a problem of eliminating small numbers of unsatisfactory teachers, this is less a matter of identification, but of developing satisfactory bureaucratic procedures that are acceptable to the profession as a whole. Other purposes of teacher appraisal include promotion and merit pay. How far is it possible and desirable to use teacher appraisal to satisfy administrative purposes remains a highly contentious question[3].

Where the major purpose of teacher appraisal is professional development, then the following sequential procedures have been usefully deployed: a preliminary discussion with the teacher involved, classroom observation of the teacher in action, a post-observation discussion, and an agreed plan for future professional development in the context of a particular school. As discussed below, teacher appraisal of this sort is part of a larger process of school-based review. These sequential procedures would need to be modified the more successful that a school has been in adopting a team-teaching approach.

The question of *who* should appraise teachers is closely related to its purpose and is an area of potential controversy. In some countries, inspectors play a large part in the appraisal; generally, however, appraisal is regarded as part of the responsibility of senior teachers, with the principal appraising those immediately subordinate to him or her. This assumes, of course, hierarchical relations within school staffs that are not typical of all OECD countries. To achieve effective appraisal requires careful training[4]. For example, all principals and other appraisers could profit from attending a training course followed by updating every year. Ideally, all staff should also be prepared for appraisal by means of an induction course designed to point out its benefits as well as clarifying the procedures involved. It is also evident that to appraise fairly and effectively requires more than one period of classroom observation; one study has recommended between eight and twelve hours' appraisal time per teacher. Clearly the cost involved is considerable, but then, monitoring and quality control are highly expensive. Hence the temptation to rely instead on questionable market mechanisms.

For teacher appraisal to be successful, the school climate is all-important. A tradition of institutional self-evaluation and constructive self-criticism is regarded by some as a prerequisite since only in such conditions will there be a climate of trust between appraiser and appraised. It is also necessary for teachers to be involved in the development of the appraising scheme rather than have it imposed upon them. Schemes that employ more than one appraiser gain in reliability and validity, but increase the costs considerably. Experience in industry had shown the value of using ipsative scales — that is, asking appraisers to compare the performance of an individual on one dimension with his or her performance on other dimensions to indicate relative strengths and weaknesses rather than his or her approximation to norms.

However the results of the appraisal are used, it is arguable that teachers as well as parents and policy-makers need tighter definitions of professional competence, for parents as a prerequisite of accountability, for teachers as a component of professional status. In reality, the full implications of the principle of appraisal for professional development are rarely acknowledged or put into operation: one of the most important features of appraisal is that the appraiser should diagnose the needs of the teacher being appraised in terms of desirable courses, study leave, and other, possibly expensive, recommendations. If teachers are expected to take professional development seriously then such recommendations should be implemented. Frequently they are ignored, and cynical attitudes to the appraisal process quickly set in. Thus, a teacher who has attended many courses and been frequently assessed is scarcely likely to be content if there is no scope for promotion. There is a dilemma here, therefore: to be viewed primarily as an instrument of professional development, appraisal cannot be too closely tied to career rewards or sanctions, yet positive appraisals from which no change occurs at all may prove to be equally unacceptable to teachers.

SCHOOL-BASED EVALUATION

Some authorities consider that teacher appraisal is best seen in the context of school-based evaluation. Others point out that both school self-evaluation and the appraisal of individual teachers share common prerequisites in terms of the institutional climate. Good morale within the school is important as well as a commitment to appraisal and acting on results. School-based evaluation is defined as a process by which teachers discuss their own school as a group of professionals in such a way as to improve the quality of education. It is now being developed in a number of OECD countries as a critical key for appraising quality[5].

School ethos

Some researchers have devised indicators of school "ethos" objectively and have found that it is a major variable in distinguishing between schools in terms of pupil performance[6]. Such indicators include examination results, retention rates, truancy rates, teacher absence, pupil crime rates, extra-curricular activities, and links with the community. Self-evaluation includes discussion of school ethos and climate in terms of whether the school in question is welcoming or hostile, democratic or autocratic, organised or chaotic, stimulating or inhibiting, attractive or dull. Usually, no attempt is made to measure these features but they may be a useful way of encouraging teachers to think about their own school as the first step towards adopting positive changes. There is growing interest in attempting to measure these and other aspects of school life, and to develop performance indicators at the school level. In France and Japan research projects are examining methods for aggregating teachers' opinions on their own schools and applying what is termed a "School Management Diagnosis Card"[7].

As pointed out in Chapter 4, one of the points of general agreement is the desirability of schools reaching consensus on curriculum objectives. This principle holds true in all countries whether or not there is a prescribed national curriculum. Any set of curriculum guidelines needs interpretation by the teachers involved, and it is always helpful for those teachers to discuss openly the translation of curriculum objectives into classroom practice and teaching methods. However, such discussions of curriculum objectives do not involve specifying objectives in behavioural terms.

Monitoring the performance of students

As a rule, teachers can profit from looking at two aspects of student performance: first, improving methods of monitoring student achievement; secondly, improving the standards of student achievement. Teachers might well be encouraged to discuss aspects of monitoring especially in terms of developing better methods of record-keeping, possibly related to national performance scores but bearing in mind the individual characteristics of the school. Most schools could certainly benefit from such discussions. Similarly, standards of student achievement could be raised by discussions about improving individual and school methods of diagnosing student learning problems.

The use of resources

A frequent criticism of schools is that expensive resources are wasted or used inefficiently. In particular, there is often a lack of co-ordination between academic planning and the costing of resources. Teachers will usually find it more constructive to discuss these questions in the context of improving quality rather than cutting costs.

Reporting to parents and the local community

What most parents want is clear descriptive information about the school rather than detailed technical evaluation reports. It is important to reassure parents by demonstrating that their own aspirations for their children are not out of step with the aims of the school and the teaching methods employed. One aspect of the assessment issue underlined by this example is that there are very different information needs, as well as methods of acquiring the relevant data, depending on the audience and level of the system in question. Providing clear information of direct use to parents and pupils is different from compiling global indicators of the system's performance. These are different again from those indicators and assessments either of the "value-added" that can be attributed to an individual school or specific aspects of schooling of particular interest to teachers.

PARENTAL CHOICE

Different views about choice

It is being proposed in some quarters that the surest way of evaluating the comparative quality of schools is to place them in the position of having to compete for students as though in the market place. This entails giving parents and their children the right to choose a school that appeals to them rather than being constrained to attend a particular school. The proposal is further endorsed by the view that selecting a school for a child should not be the exclusive privilege of those parents who can afford to pay the fees charged by private schools. Advocates also claim that freedom of choice will enhance parents' involvement in the education of their children and increase educational opportunity for some poor and disadvantaged students.

Opposition to the idea of untrammelled parental choice is founded on support for community rather than individualistic concerns and the belief that an important function of public education is to transmit common cultural values of a national scope rather than to reinforce the more parochial attitudes and values of the family. It is not an altogether new conflict. In the United States, for example, the "common school" tradition has derived from a philosophy of assimilating migrants from diverse backgrounds into a common culture. That powerful tradition, however, has always jarred to some extent with the American tradition of individualism, freedom of religion, and choice in other spheres. Furthermore, in recent years migrant groups have become more vocal in their demands to retain aspects of their own cultural background and more resistant to the educational melting pot argument. Increasingly, minority groups want some aspects of their culture — notably religion and language — to be preserved, and believe that schools can play a role in transmitting and preserving their distinctive qualities as discussed at the end of Chapter 2. The competing demands of such groups have put urban schools under great strain, to such an extent that some would now question whether the common school can continue to accommodate all the demands made upon it. The "common culture" argument would, while valuing minority cultures within a society, suggest that part of the price of belonging to a society is, along with paying taxes, submitting to certain values held by the host society and reinforced by publicly-maintained schools. In several countries, this problem is often manifested by the presence of sizeable religious communities, for example, whose attitude to girls and women may be sharply contrasted with developments in the mainstream culture.

Diverse national arrangements

Private schools already exist in considerable numbers in some OECD countries. It is also well known that parents wishing to exercise choice of which school they wish their child to attend within the public system can do so by choosing to reside in a desired school attendance area. This has become a common parental practice in several countries, particularly as comprehensivisation has removed other formal distinctions between types of school, but it usually rests on being in a position to afford that option. Other opportunities for choice within public systems may exist; in certain parts of the United States these include alternative schools, magnet schools, open enrolment, limited transfer options, inter-district transfer, and the right to provide efficient education within the home.

National responses to a recent OECD enquiry[8] show a very wide range of practices as well as considerable differences in attitudes to choice. Most countries appear to make some provision for parental choice on religious grounds, with or without government financial support. Some countries, such as Ireland, the Netherlands, and Spain, operate a system in which a large proportion of schools is private but state-supported. In the Netherlands, this policy is, however, accompanied by a complementary policy of positive discrimination: for example, inner-city schools are given more support to compensate for particular problems. In England and Wales, independent (private) schools cater for only about 6 per cent of the population, but their influence is much greater than that figure would suggest, since students from those schools are heavily over-represented in universities and prestigious occupations. A minority of students in private schools is supported by the State, and the percentage was increased after 1980 by the Assisted Places Scheme. New legislation for schools passed in 1988 extends significantly the role of parents in the decision-making and running of schools, in addition to extended room for the exercise of parental choice between schools.

Counter-arguments on the choice issue are often forcefully expressed in the Nordic countries. These arguments tend to rest on a philosophy of education that places great emphasis on equity and the social functions of compulsory education. So far as the purpose of education is to transmit a common culture and national traditions, then the expansion of choice and the increase of variety between schools may militate against schooling as a socially cohesive institution. In Norway, finance is deliberately geared to creating schools that are, as far as possible, of equal quality and there is no encouragement of competition between them. The belief is that genuine choice possibilities can only be secured if quality differences are avoided. The choice will then be made according to criteria such as closeness to home. Advocates of the common culture approach, including many American educators, argue that the major task of public education is to be concerned, through a system of common schools, with the transmission of values, knowledge, and skills to all, leaving minority aspects of culture to choices within the school curriculum or to be provided by the family and other groups outside schools. It is interesting that in the OECD survey of the choice issue, Norway and Finland provided examples of countries where, although the size of the sector is very small, private schools do receive full public support at levels equal to the maintained sector. The Scandinavian tradition of strong support for the state education system goes hand in hand with generous financial backing for independent schools so long as they meet defined standards of adequacy.

Choice as the route to quality

It is well established that close parental involvement in their children's schooling has a positive effect on both attainment and on the school. In this regard, it is not easy to refute the argument that parental choice will improve attainment. The issue remains how that choice is exercised and how widely opportunities are availed of. Proponents of greater freedom of parental choice are obliged to face up to real potential difficulties and any education authority that takes up the issue cannot avoid addressing three central questions raised in the OECD synthesis of national statements on choice of schools[9]:

— How far does the explicit encouragement of diversity and competition among schools conflict with the socialisation of all children into a common cultural heritage where each is entitled to a high-quality schooling?
— Does the present evidence suggest that the degree to which parents exercise choice favours the privileged over the less privileged?
— If parents exercise rights to choose more extensively, leading to sharper divides between desired (and hence popular) schools and less desired or discredited schools, what problems does this create not only for the latter category but for the popular schools too?

The reality remains that in democratic societies some parents will always find ways and means of exercising choice. Education systems can best face that reality by encouraging each school to develop its own strengths. On this basis, parents and children choose the school that suits them best, thereby respecting the democratic principle and engaging schools in constructive competition. This assumes that no part of the system is allowed unfair advantage in that competition and that extra assistance be given to schools in districts suffering marked disadvantages.

EVALUATION OF THE WHOLE SYSTEM

Just as every school needs to keep its student assessment and self-evaluation procedures under critical review, so an education authority at any level needs to have some means of evaluating the effectiveness of its policies, receiving feedback from the schools and, where necessary, guidance towards changes in policy. Countries differ in the way that policy-makers are kept in touch with classroom practices and standards. Civil servants, school superintendents, regional advisers, and national inspectors may or may not be involved. In democratic societies, the process of evaluation and accountability is essentially two-way: the central or regional authorities need to have adequate channels of communication to inform schools about policy decisions, but the policy-makers must also be sensitive to the views of teachers and parents. Similarly, the policy-makers need to have reliable information about attainment levels in schools, and to be constantly reassured about the different aspects that are seen to comprise quality, before they can realistically plan future developments. Significantly, in most countries the evaluation and monitoring of the whole system are increasingly being observed and commented upon by the general public, by representatives of the mass media, and by interest groups or "powerful voices" such as employers, who are no longer prepared to be silent spectators. This, as outlined in Chapter 1, is one major reason behind the emergence of the quality issue in its contemporary form.

There is no agreement among countries on the need for national assessment based on systematic surveys, but there is an increasing consensus on the necessity of having adequate information on a national basis about how well the system performs in terms of the different components of quality and standards. Economic indicators are needed to demonstrate cost-effectiveness, and even more important are quality indicators. Some feel that it is very important to have national data on the different components of quality, preferably in a form that facilitates international comparison, so that much speculation and hearsay can be countered. In the rest of this chapter, we take up two major aspects of assessment and monitoring of school systems — inspectorates and statistics and indicators.

The role of central inspectorates

One of the ways in which national monitoring can be put into operation is by employing a national force of inspectors[10]. While not all countries have central inspectorates, and some clearly have no intention of establishing one, it is accepted that most of the monitoring tasks customarily performed by inspectors must be carried out by one means or another:

— ensuring that statutory regulations are observed;
— reporting and making recommendations to the minister or responsible authority on particular schools or particular curricular developments;
— promoting the improvement of education through consultation;
— planning and taking part in in-service education and training for groups of teachers and school leaders;
— leading and inspiring curriculum development in a subject or an area of the curriculum;
— assisting in the implementation of policy decisions;
— judging the performance of individual teachers periodically;

— being an appeal authority for parents and students with complaints about their treatment.

Not all these tasks are applicable to all countries having central inspectorates.

Independence is of critical importance. Although inspectors cannot distance themselves from government policies, even when they have doubts about their efficacy, it is nevertheless essential that they retain freedom from political interference on all professional matters. It is also desirable for them to retain independence from the bureaucratic machinery so far as possible, by having, for example, the right of direct access to policy-makers. Naturally this professional status of inspectors must rest on up-to-date, first-hand knowledge of what is happening in the schools: regular visiting and inspecting of schools is, therefore, an indispensable duty.

Central and regional inspectorates can, then, perform a vital role in evaluation and monitoring whole education systems. It is to be noted, however, that teachers usually respond more favourably to a visitor offering advice, that is, to an adviser, than to someone whose title suggests formal inspection and criticism.

Statistics and indicators: national and international

Many countries concur that part of the process of improving quality in education is to make available national and international data on various aspects of educational standards. This depends, of course, on knowing what standards are, being able to measure them, and ensuring that the means do not distort the ends. It is always difficult to know whether standards are rising or falling, or how they compare with another country, unless an adequate data base exists. Some countries which rejected the notion of data collection twenty years ago are now analysing national statistics themselves and are seeking relevant international statistics on education.

The United States Department of Education has found its own data, such as that provided from the National Assessment of Educational Progress (NAEP), extremely useful at several levels and for a variety of purposes. State Governors are looking for data that are state representative and there is increasing interest in developing inter-state comparative statistics and indicators[11]. There is also a need for data presented in such a way as to be more comprehensible to the general public. Several other countries have followed the example set by the United States with NAEP. The Netherlands and Sweden have embarked on a programme of monitoring pupils' achievement; in England and Wales the Assessment of Performance Unit (APU) has existed since 1975, and Scotland has a parallel programme; France, having become dissatisfied with traditional national measurements during the 1970s, has also started to collect data on a more systematic basis. After experiments on a national basis in the 1970s, Australia has pulled back from continuation of a programme at the national level[12].

The information from surveys in providing a detailed picture of pupil performance of a kind which has not hitherto been available reveals a complex pattern of performance. Analysis goes beyond the identification of tasks which pupils find difficult, and begins to explore the nature of the difficulty. APU findings in England also point to common errors. The Unit has evidence indicating that many pupils have a poor grasp of ideas and processes once believed to be easy. Thus, the findings show that many pupils have not mastered procedural skills such as making notes or measuring and estimating. In certain other areas, pupils have done better than expected, for example in attempting practical investigations and picking out the general sense from extended texts in a foreign language. It is claimed that the work of the APU had uncovered blockages to learning, some of which might be crucial because their removal could allow pupils to move towards higher achievement. It seems from APU tests, for example, that many pupils cannot measure accurately; if that blockage could be removed, pupils could achieve more in later work in science and technology. A further beneficial spin-off of national assessment can be that the very process of constructing tests can help clarify the curricular questions of what should be taught and learned in different disciplines and the testing material may be used by individual teachers and schools. National measurement instruments, in other words, may have valuable local application.

Some express caution about national assessment. One warning is that sections of the school population that are low-achievers may suffer further if national norms are established and their performance measured against these norms and that there are crucial value questions, not just technical problems, involved in the setting up of national machinery for student assessment as discussed in Chapter 3. It is a question of what the norms are — average, minimum, age-related — and how they are used. At the end of Chapter 3, the interest in developing indicators, national and international, was underlined. There is an increasing call to have more information on such matters as the content of the curriculum, the allocations for curriculum areas, courses offered and taken at various age levels, teacher tasks, conditions of service, and training, as well as the achievement data provided by national assessment surveys. New work has begun on the development of indicators in CERI under five broad themes:

— Enrolments, educational career paths, and leavers at different stages;
— Student outcomes;
— The ecology of schools;
— Costs and resources;
— Attitudes and expectations.

It is, of course, too soon to announce any concrete results from these recent initiatives. But the re-emergence of interest in educational indicators at the international level is an illustration of the widespread interest in, and concern about, quality in schooling — the subject of this report.

The issues raised herein provide a vital component of the overall debate on quality but evaluation and monitoring are not ends in themselves. They only have value if the results they provide have an impact on improving educational practice. There is much scope for the dissemination of national educational data which could be discussed comparatively. There is a need for key personnel, such as inspectors, to meet to exchange views and information on a regular basis. There is a need for regular meetings of experts in measurement and evaluation. Much of the research being conducted on a national basis deserve to have much wider coverage, both in terms of the techniques being used and the application of the findings to other countries.

NOTES AND REFERENCES

1. Department of Education and Science (1985), *Quality in Schools: Evaluation and Appraisal*, HMSO, London. p. 7.
2. Erba, D., Coti, A., Delucchi, M. (1985), *Innovations pédagogiques au Tessin en 1985*, Institut romand de recherches et de documentation pédagogiques, Cahier du GCR No. 11, IRDP/R 85.03, Neuchâtel. Discussed in Cardinet, J. (1986), "Evaluation at Primary School Level" (OECD working document).
3. For recent reviews of the "merit pay" idea from the United States, see Alexander, K. and Monk, D.H. (eds.) (1987), *Attracting and Compensating America's Teachers* (Eighth Annual Yearbook of the American Education Finance Association), Ballinger, Cambridge, Mass.
4. See Wilson J.D., Thomson, G.O.B., Millward, B. and Keenan, T. (eds.) (1989), *Assessment for Teacher Development* (Proceedings of an International Seminar, Edinburgh, Scotland, June 1987), Falmer, London. For an earlier discussion based on U.S. literature see Darling-Hammond, L. *et al.* (1983), "Teacher Evaluation in the Organisational Context: A Review of the Literature", *Review of Educational Research*, Vol. 53. No. 3, pp. 285-328.
5. This has been a prominent area in the work of the International School Improvement Project (ISIP). See Hopkins, D. (1985), *School-based Review for School Improvement: A Preliminary State of the Art*, ISIP, OECD/CERI, ACCO, Leuven; Bollen, R. and Hopkins, D. (1987), *School-based Review: Towards a Praxis* (same publisher).
6. For example, Rutter, M. *et al.* (1979), *Fifteen Thousand Hours*, Open Books.
7. Papers presented in Ministère de l'Education nationale (forthcoming), *Evaluations et indicateurs des systèmes éducatifs* (proceedings of the joint French authorities/OECD international conference, Poitiers, 21-23 March, 1988), Paris.
8. Lines, P.M. (1986), "Parental Choice in the United States" (OECD working document), and national statements for Australia, Belgium, Denmark, Finland, Germany (including special reference to Bavaria), Ireland, Japan, Luxembourg, New Zealand, Norway, Portugal, Sweden, Switzerland, and the United Kingdom (OECD working documents).
9. OECD (1987), "Choice of Schools: A Guide to the Documentation" (OECD working documents).
10. A specific CERI activity has been devoted to examining the role of central inspectorates and to encouraging exchange of experience between them. This section draws on that work.
11. For example, the annual federal statistical publication: *The Condition of Education* has been recently substantially restyled around a series of indicators. See Center for Education Statistics (1987), *The Condition of Education: A Statistical Report*, Office of Educational Research and Improvement, U.S. Department of Education, Washington D.C.
12. See Education Research and Development Committee (1982), *National Assessment in Australia: An Evaluation of the Australian Studies in Student Performance Project*, ERDC Report No. 35, Australian Government Publishing Service, Canberra.

Chapter 8

THE RESOURCES DIMENSION

QUANTITY AND QUALITY INTERACTIONS

Common sense would seem to indicate that there ought to be a correlation between the quantity of resources allocated to schools and the educational outcomes attained in terms of specified indicators. A quick reading of the evidence, however, is not reassuring. To begin with, much depends on the appropriateness of the resources made available and the way in which they are deployed. More importantly, even if one accepts the utility of the input-output formulation (though in Part One it was suggested that, to some extent, perspectives on quality derive from the need to go beyond input-output models to focus more closely on process) it is difficult to come by compelling empirical evidence that shows a strong correlation between inputs and outputs even as measured by standardized achievement in tests. As for non-cognitive outcomes, which may be considered just as desirable as cognitive ones, they have so far proved almost impossible to measure; still less is it possible to demonstrate their relation to resources.

A comprehensive worldwide review by Angus *et al.*[1] on the effects of resources on student achievement suggests there is no universal law relating the two. From this they do not infer that increases in resources make no difference. It is, rather, that the way resources are used and the environments of schools can vary so greatly that global quantitative analyses are unlikely to show consistent effects. They do suggest that the use of time in schools (see Chapter 6) appears to be a variable of considerable importance in explaining student outcomes. But it is not just the availability of more time but how time is spent that is significant. Increases in resources which permit, for example, reductions in class size may provide the possibility of improved outcomes, but they are not a sufficient precondition of improvement. There are two points here: global correlations are unlikely to reveal much about specific cases of good practice and efficiency since the level of analysis used is simply too aggregate; numerous different combinations of the "inputs" of schooling are possible for any given "output level", ruling out any simple relationship between resources and achievement levels.

Yet many politicians and educationists are fully persuaded that the educational expansion of the 1960s and early 1970s, when weighed against positive achievements, has led to an intolerable amount of waste of resources and that specific school regions and districts have been demonstrably extravagant. For example, it is alleged that there is overstaffing of administrators and teachers and that the available books and learning aids are not being used at all or used wrongly. The general judgement may well be an inspired guess but it is not founded on empirical evidence. The judgement about specific school districts and schools, however, can appear to draw telling corroboration from the fact that some districts and schools really do spend more than others without showing comparable gains.

One major problem with making a quick judgement based on spending and achievement levels alone, however, is that they tend to leave largely out of account another correlation, namely, that between unsatisfactory or below-average outcomes and the poor socio-economic background of students, which remains the key predictor of educational achievement. When that variable has been allowed for, the comparative findings become of questionable validity. Assessment of the school's contribution and use of resources requires attention to the "value-added" factor as discussed in Chapter 3.

It may be argued that, in any case, the search for an input-output equation is purely academic since, in practice, governments today have to impose a cap or ceiling at a certain prescribed level on public educational expenditure. For many OECD countries, that ceiling represents the one reached six to ten years ago or, indeed, for some countries, long before that. Governments can then claim that they would be only glad to allocate a bigger percentage of GNP on public expenditure to education but simply cannot afford to do so in view of other national obligations. They can also choose to align themselves with critics of the alleged continuing wastage or inefficient use of educational allocations by arguing that qualitative improvement can and must be brought about by the efficient deployment of existing resources. In other words, schools are today exhorted to "give better value for money".

The previous Federal Minister of Education in Australia put that argument in terms that were blunt but that have been echoed by other OECD Ministers of Education:

"The Commonwealth Government is no longer prepared to pour buckets of money into the education system in an indiscriminate manner. It wants to know where its money is going and what the expenditure on education is achieving. If the education systems insist that is not possible, then I'm afraid the Federal Government may have to look at other areas of activity to direct its limited funds[2]".

It may be added that allegations of waste or inefficiency in the use of educational resources reflect a widespread sentiment in some OECD countries that management across all sectors of public expenditure, not only education, has tended to be wasteful, if not profligate.

So the reality is that most education systems cannot hope to obtain significantly greater public resources, yet at the same time they are under pressure to demonstrate that they are extracting full value from those that already exist. It is important to stress that imperative because, ironically, most of the specific recommendations offered for improving quality, as opposed to those that are couched in normative terms, postulate increased expenditure, often on a large scale. This is notably true of proposals to modify teacher recruitment and training policies. The aims of recruiting better-qualified teachers and teachers of subjects where there is a shortage are unlikely to be realised without offering higher starting salaries and better career incentives. More and better in-service training provision costs additional money to provide. Similarly, devoting more care to the appointment of principals and school leaders and making sure that they are properly trained and kept up-to-date professionally also entail additional expenditure. Systematic curricular development within schools absorbs more teacher time and, hence, more teachers. Extending the school day and school year also requires more teacher time and, therefore, more expenditure. This point needs to be underlined: paradoxically, most of the specific recommendations for improving the quality of schooling, *including those often proposed by value-for-money advocates*, postulate increased expenditure on a large scale. Whatever room there undoubtedly is for more efficient use of resources, the potential costliness of reform cannot be dismissed with the blanket call for greater efficiency.

The search for efficiency

Stating that is not to deny the obvious need for the efficient use of available resources: are there any ways of improving schooling without increasing costs? Four general proposals in vogue are *a)* to deploy staff and resources more effectively; *b)* to attract or increase parental and other external contributions; *c)* to make economies by using new instructional technologies; *d)* to rely, at least partially, on consumer preferences.

About the *rational deployment of resources* some considerations should scarcely require stating. Most obviously, it is inequitable to permit gross disparities either in resource inputs per student or in pupil/teacher ratios for similar types of school. It is bad management to tolerate overall surpluses of teachers in one area and overall shortages in others or to have surplus mathematics teachers in some schools and unqualified mathematics teachers in others. It is not acceptable for teachers to teach subjects for which they are not qualified in the sense of possessing a poor grasp of the requisite subject matter. It is unjust that some schools should have well stocked, and others poorly stocked, libraries, that some should have computers and others not. Yet all these anomalies can be identified. Above all, it is evident that, whereas in some countries there is a rough equality of expenditure across schools, in others there are glaring differences from school district to district and sometimes within the same district.

It is also true that many of the increased resources accruing during the years of educational expansion were not directed to classroom teaching. In general, measures of class size show a smaller percentage reduction than the percentage increase in resources or even the percentage reduction in pupil/teacher ratios. Some of the additional resources have gone to the appointment of auxiliary staff and to enlarging and diversifying administrative infrastructures.

Already, some schools do receive *parental support* in cash or in kind or in both. With a few significant country exceptions, this constitutes only a small percentage of the recurrent cost of running a school but it is nevertheless often sufficient to ensure a significant increase in the supply of books and equipment and to permit a greater variety of extra-curricular activities. No one in a democratic society can reasonably object to parents voluntarily giving financial support to their children's schools. A question of equity arises, however, over the financing of schools located in poor socio-economic areas. Are their existing disadvantages to be aggravated? Or does social justice require that they be allocated extra resources weighted according to the average income level of the surrounding neighbourhood? At the end of the day, an element of inequality is bound to remain because some schools will have resources above the average and cater for students drawn from an upper socio-economic background, factors that cannot apply to the system as a whole.

To resort to *new technology instruments and devices* as a form of economy is for the time being scarcely feasible. The initial investment in equipment is high; teachers have to be retrained to make good use, for example, of microcomputers; the appropriate software has to be created. In the longer term educational technology may help reduce the time teachers and administrators spend on some existing tasks, freeing them to do other tasks or to spend more time on tasks at present being imperfectly performed or to attend training courses which would otherwise occupy out-of-school time and perhaps incur additional costs. Meanwhile, introducing new technology necessarily means increased expenditure. Though many countries have now attained relatively good levels of hardware in their schools (though this still varies widely and machinery is always subject to obsolescence), retraining and software remain inadequate in most places and the availability and use of other technologies such as interactive videos will necessarily entail significant new expenditures.

The *introduction of consumer preferences* is now under consideration in a few countries as discussed in the previous chapter. This would entail the de-zoning of schools so that parents could choose to send their children to whichever school they wish and resources would follow the pupil rather than be tied closely to each school. The assumption is that schools with a bad name will be avoided and eventually close down for lack of resources if they fail to acquire a good reputation whereas effective schools will flourish. In other words, the market is left to determine what is good and what is bad. The arguments around these policy directions have been orchestrated above. We would simply add here the difficulty that "bad" schools tend to be congregated in deprived areas and that many parents really have no choice but to send their children to the nearest school. Furthermore, in several countries, many parents already exercise consumer preference by sending their children to private as opposed to public or state schools.

It is essential to record that some education authorities, national, regional, and local, fully recognise that improving quality does require greater resources. Thus, several countries have opted not to make savings from falling enrolments but to put the resources saved into qualitative improvements. In the United States, in the wake of the numerous national reports on the condition of education, a number of states have sharply raised teachers' salaries. We would also draw attention to this statement from a report prepared by the Committee for Economic Development, a United States independent research and educational organisation, remarkable because this body is made up of two hundred *business executives* as well as educators:

> "Many of the specific reforms we advocate will require increasing our present level of investment in education. Although resources at all levels of government are being constrained, we believe that the nation is underinvesting in public education. A larger investment is essential and has the potential for a very significant return in both human and financial terms. With its strong stake in quality education, the business community should give increased investment in public education its wholehearted support."[3]

Guidelines on resources

Given that there is no single or simple relationship between resource inputs and educational outcomes, education authorities must rely on pragmatic policies. This implies ensuring that:

i) at every level, all the actors in the education system become cost-conscious, strive to make economies wherever possible, and ensure that resources are used where they will result in the highest possible learning gains;
ii) as a corollary, public expenditure must be fully accounted for;
iii) increased allocations should go only to well-designed reforms for which clear goals have been set and convincing strategies for implementation worked out;

- *iv)* all those in responsible positions, whether they be administrators, principals or school leaders, or school board members, must be trained to manage resources efficiently;
- *v)* schools should receive approximately equal resources per student;
- *vi)* schools with special problems or serving special groups should receive additional resources;
- *vii)* every school should have a minimum supply of learning resources, notably textbooks and writing materials;
- *viii)* all teaching and administrative personnel must be effectively deployed;
- *ix)* wherever appropriate, parental or other outside contributions should be encouraged;
- *x)* the physical fabric and environment of each school should be conducive to learning.

APPROPRIATE PHYSICAL RESOURCES

The last recommendation is elaborated on in some depth below because:

- *a)* it concerns an indispensable resource;
- *b)* it is too easily taken for granted;
- *c)* there has been recently a significant slump in capital expenditure shares of education budgets in many OECD countries;
- *d)* it is one resource element, at least as demonstrated by an OECD special programme, Decentralised Programme on Educational Building (PEB), about which some positive evidence across a number of this family of countries is available.

There is a further reason for focusing especially on physical, rather than financial, resources in this chapter. Financial arrangements are exceedingly complex both within and across countries. Not only are rapid summaries of such arrangements impossible, but it is extremely difficult to isolate examples that are directly relevant to quality *per se* as opposed to elaborating cases that illustrate particular financial arrangements.

Adequate physical provision

The physical reality of school buildings is an essential element in all education systems. Their layout and the equipment in them together represent a fundamental input to the educational process. In the majority of OECD countries, the cost of maintaining and running the physical facilities for education typically accounts for 15 to 20 per cent of total recurrent expenditure. Moreover, there are several countries still facing substantial demand for new buildings to house pupils in the compulsory age group. As with financial resources, the link between buildings and the quality of the education provided therein is by no means simple or direct. Many adults are apt to recall teachers who coped superbly despite overcrowded or noisy classrooms in dilapidated or under-equipped schools. Some can teach well in a bad building, just as some will teach badly in a good one. But, all things being equal, good facilities do contribute to effective learning whereas poor facilities affect educational outcomes adversely in a number of different ways.

The contribution made by the particular combination of size, style, condition and configuration of spaces that constitutes a school is often underestimated, if not by architects then at least by educational theorists. Nonetheless, recent statements, such as those from HMI in England, are forthright. Holding that there is indeed "a statistically significant association between the quality of work and the appropriateness of the accommodation available"[4], HMI has reported that:

> "Many pupils and teachers are having to work in accommodation which is inappropriate and does not offer a decent working environment. One clear consequence of this is that the quality of work and the standards achieved by pupils are adversely affected."[5]

The inspectors noted the well-known expedient of cutting back on building maintenance, redecoration, and the replacement of furniture when funds are insufficient, and warned that if the deficiencies were not quickly remedied, conditions would deteriorate further. It is instructive to compare their judgement with that expressed in an earlier report by the Department of Education and Science:

> "In general the fabric of school buildings is in good condition and schools are not unsafe or unhealthy places. On most of the criteria chosen for analysis the majority of school buildings are satisfactory, but there is a substantial minority of schools — mainly older ones — with extensive and often severe deficiencies in their fitness for educational purposes, and gross deficiencies in amenity, by today's standards."[6]

It is not the purpose here to analyse the specific situation described in those two declarations, but to point out the link that is identified between aspects of quality of facilities and quality of education, and to attempt to draw out certain of the different elements which contribute to satisfactory physical conditions. As above, it would be a fool's errand to seek to identify a rigid relationship between inputs and outputs, especially as a survey carried out by OECD's PEB has revealed that the very poverty of relevant data makes analysis difficult. It is possible, however, to look at particular elements of the complex compound and to reach some conclusions. For example, it is perfectly possible at the local level to make an assessment of the expenditure required to maintain buildings properly. If actual expenditure repeatedly falls short of this amount there is no doubt that quality will deteriorate. The message from a recent PEB seminar on building maintenance involving participants from thirteen OECD countries was unequivocal: funds for the maintenance of educational buildings were insufficient; the professionals concerned found themselves unable to present a sufficiently convincing case for their increase to those responsible for resource allocation; there was a marked deterioration in the condition of educational buildings and in the morale of their users; there was an increasing risk of severe disruption[7]. Thus, whatever the conception and design of a school building, its proper maintenance is essential and neglect will, sooner or later, affect the educational process, quite apart from making bad economic sense and creating a potential danger to safety and security.

Minimum standards

Given, then, that the school building is a critical aspect of the educational process, what are the significant constituents of satisfactory provision? Three groups of factors can be distinguished:

— "health and safety factors" that concern the well-being of the building's users;
— "environmental" factors that are conducive to good education in a general sense;
— "curriculum-related" factors that are conducive to effective teaching and learning in specific ways.

The first group, health and safety factors, although in some respects the most important, is the least controversial and the least relevant to the quality debate. No one questions the need for fire precautions or safe storage of dangerous equipment. Everyone agrees that schools must be kept clean. New and urgent issues can arise such as recognition that blue asbestos is a danger and must be eradicated. The question is not "whether?" preventive action should be taken but "how?" or "at what cost?". Problems can arise when security requirements conflict with pedagogical or aesthetic considerations. At present, a growing number of authorities are reporting concern about vandalism which, if not strictly a "health and safety" matter, does have much to do with the well-being of a building's users. This is not the place to discuss its causes, but if the measures taken to prevent it result in restrictions on access to a school or an atmosphere of restraint, then harm may be done to the educational process. More obviously, vandalism that is unchecked can present physical dangers.

The "environmental" factors concern requirements for heating, lighting, noise reduction, ventilation, and size. The first four of these have some similarities with the factors mentioned above, and the basic argument is over, for example, what adequate standards of noise control might be, rather than about the need to reduce noise at all. But even in these areas there can be disagreement. Thus, one commentator[8] identifies a different appreciation of the value of natural ventilation and natural light as a prime factor why some reject the North American model of an open-plan school with a rigorously controlled internal environment. Advances in knowledge can also cause perceptions to change, and we are witnessing increasing concern about indoor air pollution now that energy conservation consciousness has seen to it that many rooms are virtually draught-proof. Normal practice in these areas is to specify minimum standards designed as much to ensure the avoidance of the extravagant as the availability of the essential.

It is the fifth of these environmental factors, size, which has attracted most attention among school planners. At one time, most OECD countries laid down space standards, either specifying minima *and* maxima or, more simply, minima, and these standards expressed what was considered to be necessary for the proper functioning of the schools concerned. They had also, usually, the second objective of restraining the cost of making the necessary provision. It was striking, however, that despite international agreement on the principle of norms, the actual standards imposed varied considerably from country to country[9]. There was some correlation between national wealth (GNP per capita) and space standards, which supports the common-sense hypothesis that more generous space standards are educationally desirable, within reasonable limits. However, not all the variation can be explained on this basis.

In recent years, there has been a general tendency to decentralise responsibility for educational building and this has resulted in a corresponding relaxation as norms become recommendations, and recommendations become advice. Reliable data across countries on the effect of this change on areas being built are not available, although it is certainly the case that expenditure constraints have had the effect of pushing these towards the minimum. On the other hand, where school rolls are falling and schools are operating below their designed capacity, the smaller number of pupils will usually expand into the available space, and the actual area in use per pupil may well be higher than hitherto. Under-used schools are today a more prevalent problem than overcrowded ones.

Development work among school architects has concentrated on improving the ratio of teaching area to total area by reducing "unnecessary" circulation or other space. The prime motivation for such work would usually have been to make the most effective use of existing resources and thus aim to improve the quality of education provided at a given cost. To our knowledge, no international study concerned with the quality of education has sought to relate that to the teaching areas provided, an exercise which runs into the serious difficulty of separating out the effect of the building from the other factors involved in the process. Area standards, such as they are, remain based on traditional practice, modified by economic necessity, rather than educational theory.

It is the final group of factors, those described above as "curriculum-related", that are the most contentious. The questions are no longer of the type "how much can we afford?" but "what arrangement should we choose?" They concern the organisation of schools, both internal and external — what is the appropriate size for a school? What size should teaching groups be? What specialist accommodation is required? Should an open plan be adopted? Questions such as these move the argument on from minimum standards to the educational aims and assumptions underlying the design of the school; they concern appropriateness as well as adequacy.

Educational aims

Keywords in the debate about buildings in recent years have been "flexibility" — the characteristic of a building that permits variation in learning activities, class size, and teaching style — and "adaptability" — the characteristic of a building that makes it simple to adapt physically. These two characteristics were already identified by the OECD over a decade ago as critical to meeting educational aims while achieving value for money[10]. Flexibility and adaptability in practice should have meant the provision of a mix of general activity areas and single-purpose ("committed") space, complemented by mobile furniture and equipment, laid out in a building which avoids complex lighting, ventilation and circulation patterns. Single-storey buildings were recommended where possible, using a structural frame which would offer the possibility of a range of spans or structural layouts, and with space left on the site for future extensions.

Such flexibility and adaptability cannot be created in a vacuum; the educational policy of the school, and the attitudes of the individuals concerned, must also be taken into account, as discussed in the next section. Too often, theoretical models have been foisted on teachers, and too often "flexibility" has been interpreted as a barren openness. Partly as a result of this, disputes have arisen between the proponents and the detractors of "open-plan" education, particularly where these were seen, or intended, not as neutral, but as changing the way in which teaching is carried out. On the question of whether open-space school designs as such affect educational performance for good or ill, the research remains inconclusive[11].

It is possible to go further than this. Many activities need special accommodation and equipment if they are to be properly catered for — the sciences, many vocational subjects, music, art, and drama, have long been recognised as having specific requirements. The need to introduce rapidly into education systems adequate provision for computing is currently presenting considerable difficulties, and many are the makeshift solutions which are being adopted. All these things add to the cost and complexity of educational building, but education can be impoverished if they are neglected.

The importance of making suitable provision becomes very clear when the needs of those who are physically handicapped are considered. As integration of the disabled into ordinary schools continues, more attention must be paid to what are often quite straightforward and seemingly unimportant details of design, but which, if overlooked, can lead to irritation and sometimes danger. There is no shortage of good advice, but the task of implementing it in the stock of existing buildings is considerable.

One further aspect which has often been overlooked in the past, and whose influence on the efficiency of the teaching and learning process is becoming appreciated, is what may be termed learning support areas. Included under this heading would be staffrooms, preparation areas, space for storage and maintenance of equipment, and social areas.

The school as an entity

The size of a school, the age range for which it caters, and the education system under which it operates are in principle decided on educational grounds by policy-makers, and the building is in a sense a "neutral" element in the discussion about which arrangements are the most suitable. The buildings appropriate to whatever educational policy prevails can in theory be conceived and constructed. In practice, of course, very few schemes can start with a "green field site"; decisions are constrained by what already exists. Educational buildings can last a hundred years or more, although needs and practices will change much more rapidly. Here again, adaptability comes into its own and this will avoid the necessity to provide nothing but demountable classrooms to meet new requirements. Buildings that have been conceived to a very rigid plan are more likely to need expensive remodelling when the demands placed on them change, as they inevitably will.

That said, building economics have often hitherto dictated that only in the largest institutions can a full range of facilities (including, for example, a sports hall or a drama centre) be provided. Where buildings are conceived on a large scale, the architect, in conjunction with the school planners, can do much to humanise their scale without losing their economic and functional advantages. In this way he or she may not only avoid some of the problems of vandalism which are increasingly preoccupying administrators, but also enrich the educational experience, which is essentially a personal one. Some recent thinking in this area uses the concept of "networking", which has been opened up by recent advances in information technology, in which a number of smaller establishments, by sharing facilities, can have the advantages of a larger complex while retaining a human scale[12].

Many of the points made above are brought together in the demand for the "users" — teachers, parents, administrators, or pupils, but especially the first group — to have at their disposal the spaces they need and which they can use effectively. The best way in which to realise this is to ensure that they take a real part in the briefing process — the sequence of discussions and negotiations, formal or informal, protracted or quickly settled — which leads to decisions about the way in which a school will be built or, more frequently today, will be remodelled. Recent discussion[13] takes the prior analysis of space use to a quite sophisticated level but it remains for such an approach to become widely accepted.

Another development which has its foundations in the widespread movement towards decentralisation of educational administration concerns the way in which resources, once provided, are used and managed. This is an aspect of the role of school leaders which is often neglected[14] but where they can make a significant contribution to the life of the institution. If current trends towards devolving more financial responsibility for the resources consumed to the institutional level continue, the role of the principal or leadership group as manager will need to be taken still more seriously. The motives for such developments may be mixed, but insofar as they lead to greater job satisfaction and better running of the establishment they can be welcomed as contributing to the quality of schooling.

The education system as a whole

The concept of "networking" has been introduced in the previous section. It has a potential application not only to groups of schools but also to co-operative groupings of schools or all educational institutions, and human service provision. A number of innovative schemes in the 1960s and 1970s sought to integrate on one site educational, sporting, cultural, and community health facilities, but most of these consisted of expensive new developments for which there are now few opportunities. The economic case for joint use and provision of some educational and other social facilities remains strong, however, and the creation of more or less formal networks may be the way forward. Some of the most interesting experiments now taking place are in post-compulsory and adult education and it is often the new management arrangements created which are critical to their success. Insofar as they open up opportunities and improve access they can make a particularly valuable contribution[15].

A final consideration concerns less the school buildings in themselves, but the way in which they are put to use. Most OECD countries still operate a three-term year with a very long summer break, based on the needs of nineteenth-century agrarian societies. Several experiments aimed at increasing the amount of time for which buildings are in use have demonstrated the substantial economies that can be made[16]. The reorganisation of school time can also be done in such a way as to open up new teaching opportunities and to give pupils the chance to learn at their own pace. Other social and educational benefits have been claimed for several different ways of arranging the school day and the school year as discussed in Chapter 6 above.

Concluding remarks on physical resources

This discussion shows that while it may not be possible to quantify the effect on educational output of changes to the built resources provided, the impact of buildings on the teaching and learning process is substantial and many-faceted. Of the factors outlined above, some contribute to the basic comfort and safety of teachers and pupils, and others are concerned with making the learning process more effective in itself. It should not be forgotten, however, that any improvement in the effectiveness of decision-making and management in educational buildings can be expected to lead to economies which will lead, directly or indirectly, to improvements in education; every penny spent unnecessarily on heating or air-conditioning, just to take examples, detracts from expenditure on teachers or books.

There is, finally, one argument that has not yet been fully brought out. The quality of education, however defined, is in some way linked with the morale of teachers, pupils, parents, and administrators. A proper investigation of the concept of morale belongs to the realms of psychology but insofar as it is dependent on such factors as the feeling of control over one's environment, a sense of progress, and identification with personal space, it is clear that the school building has much to contribute to it. A physical environment which does nothing to evoke a warm, caring sense and welcoming atmosphere will do little to promote the quality of education.

NOTES AND REFERENCES

1. Angus, M.J. et al. (1983), *Setting Standards for School Resources: the Contribution of Research*, Commonwealth Schools Commission Target, Recurrent Resource Standards Study Discussion Paper No. 2, Canberra.

2. Opening address by the then Minister of Education, Senator Susan Ryan, to the Third National Conference of the Australian Curriculum Studies Association, Melbourne, 1985.

3. Committee for Economic Development (1985), *Investing in our Children*, New York. p. 37.

4. Department of Education and Science (1986), *Report by Her Majesty's Inspectors on the Effects of Local Authority Expenditure Policies on Education Provision in England - 1985*, HMSO, London, para. 60.

5. *Ibid:* para. 62.

6. Department of Education and Science and Welsh Office (1977), *A Study of School Building*, HMSO, London, para. 7.4.

7. OECD/PEB (1986), "The Maintenance of Educational Buildings: Policies and Strategies", Paris (document for general distribution).

8. Maclure, S. (1984), *Educational Development and School Building: Aspects of Public Policy 1945-73*, Longman, Harlow.

9. OECD/PEB (1976), "Analytical Survey of Current Norms for School Building", Paris (internal document).

10. OECD/PEB (1976), *Providing for Future Change: Adaptability and Flexibility in School Building*, Paris.

11. See, for example, Weinstein, C.S. (1979), "The Physical Environment of the School: A Review of the Research", *Review of Educational Research* (Fall).

12. Mayfield, J. (1986), "Schools as part of a network of learning facilities: implications for educational building". Discussion paper for a PEB symposium of that title held in Segovia, Spain, December 1986.

13. For example, Solvang, R. and Strommen, S. (1988), "Assessing space requirements and space use in educational buildings", in OECD/PEB (1988). "Educational Space Requirements and the Effective Use of Resources" (Conclusions of a Seminar held in Lysebu, Voksenkollen, Norway, 20-23 May, 1986), Paris (document for general distribution).
14. Among the case studies described in Hopes, C. (ed.) (1986), *The School Leader and School Improvement*, ACCO, Leuven, only one includes specific action related to improving the physical condition of the building.
15. Gentzbittel, M. (1987), "Greater Institutional Responsibility for Educational Property Management", OECD/PEB, Paris (document for general distribution).
16. Parker, G. (1986), "Year-round schools — an example from the United States", OECD/PEB, Paris (document for general distribution).

Chapter 9

THE SCHOOL AS THE HEART OF THE MATTER

Quality and effective schooling

So far in Part Two of this report the main components of the processes of schooling have been analysed separately in relation to the pursuit of quality. We now turn to the school itself, the heart of the matter. For no amount of external decision-making, control, and planning, let it be as enlightened and sophisticated as the best education authority can contrive, offers a guarantee that all schools will perform equally well. Each school has a life of its own that precludes conformity to anything like an exact norm of behaviour and success. By common consent, it is recognised that some schools perform better than others. On the other hand, there are certain schools which, in the eyes of those inside as well as external observers, perform very badly. Merely to know what makes some schools effective and others inadequate will not suffice to metamorphose the second into the first. Knowing, however, what a school ought to aspire to is surely a necessary condition for a poor school to do better. For that reason we propose in this final chapter to discuss, very succinctly, what is known about effective schools and how average or poor schools could be improved. Of course, it should not be deduced from this focus on the school that reforms are purely internally driven — sound public policies and adequate support mechanisms will always remain key ingredients of vitality within schools themselves.

This report has explored, as it happens, much the same ground as those educationists who, in recent times, have been propounding the idea of effective schooling and seeking through observational research to define what effectiveness implies. Indeed, we have frequently used the epithet "effective" and the very term "effective schooling". This is not surprising because schooling that is effective in terms of the pursuit of quality is the ultimate aim. It must be emphasized, however, that performance still tends to be assessed in some of the research literature exclusively by academic or cognitive achievement rather than by other variables. This could be viewed as restrictionist if it were not that the characteristics attributed to effective schools appear to be propitious for the general well-being and development of children and young people, that is, they enhance affective and social as well as cognitive development.

Still there remains a difference of approach. The idea of effective schooling comes from narrowing the focus of educational observation and research to what goes on in schools as such and to seeing if, and how, the elements that go to make up schools defined as good or effective — the adjectives tend to be used interchangeably — can be generalised. What this report has attempted, by contrast, is to look at schooling from the standpoint of education authorities or external agents with a view to applying findings to practice in individual schools. The two approaches do not conflict; ideally they should be fully complementary.

In the past, as mentioned in Chapters 1 and 6, research sought without much success to show the effects of factors that could be measured on individual or collective achievement in schools. Such factors included per-capita expenditures and class size. The conclusion tended to be that school-level variables did not seem to have a significant influence on outcomes. More recent research has amassed in-depth observations of processes in classrooms and schools and produced two important related findings: *a)* that student motivation and achievement are profoundly affected by the distinctive culture or ethos that is to be found in each school; *b)* that schools in which students perform well have essentially the same characteristics.

Characteristics of effective schools

The choice has been made of the word "characteristics" rather than, for example, "principles" of good schooling in order to avoid giving the impression that there exists some magic recipe or exact formula for the instant improvement of all schools.

Ten characteristics appear to play a particularly powerful role in determining desirable outcomes and these extend beyond good scholastic results to embrace all the aims of a school:

i)   *A commitment to clearly and commonly identified norms and goals.*

The basic premise is that each school has a distinctive ethos or culture that determines beneficially or harmfully student performance. Good schools are those that offer a climate conducive to learning. The essential prerequisite is acceptance throughout the school of common norms and goals that are clearly expressed, defined, and adhered to. This does not preclude the necessity of making it clear that, in multicultural societies, there may be a variety of possible educational goals.

ii)   *Collaborative planning, shared decision-making, and collegial work in a frame of experimentation and evaluation.*

School cohesiveness depends on the concerted actions of a teaching staff that shares responsibility for defining and maintaining whole school goals and cares for the welfare of every student. This entails good relations among all the staff, participatory decision-making and collegial management. All are committed to school improvement and to playing a part in innovation and experimentation. This presupposes that the school is not subject to rigid external prescriptions but has considerable latitude to design a part of the curriculum, to choose appropriate teaching methods, and to allocate resources with a view to achieving the best possible results.

iii) *Positive leadership in initiating and maintaining improvement.*

Leadership and the principle of collegiality are not in conflict. On the contrary, some schools are run without any hierarchical line of command. The vital consideration is that there should be efficient machinery for drawing up a whole school policy and determining who shall be responsible for providing leadership in implementing each plan and innovation whether it be as an individual or a team.

iv) Staff stability.

Schools do not function well if there are frequent staff changes or a high level of staff absenteeism. A stable staff is a precondition of a climate of security, order, and continuity. It is a precondition of managing school improvement especially during the early period of an innovation. Staff stability must be reinforced by the adjustment of teacher recruitment to the individual ethos of each school.

v) A strategy for continuing staff development related to each school's pedagogical and organisational needs.

All staff should have regular opportunities for in-service training both within the school and through external programmes. The training should be directly related to the school's actual needs. Teachers should see themselves as continually updating their knowledge and enhancing their professional skills.

vi) Working to a carefully planned and co-ordinated curriculum that ensures sufficient place for each student to acquire essential knowledge and skills.

The curriculum has to be planned in detail, including the arrangements for continuous evaluation. It should comprise a core of subject areas designed to give every student the opportunity to acquire basic knowledge and skills and to reflect the school's values.

vii) A high level of parental involvement and support.

Parents as a collective group give active support to the school in terms of voluntary services and material support. Individually, parents help motivate and support their children by complementing the school's efforts. But if parents are to be fully supportive, school doors must be welcoming to them.

viii) The pursuit and recognition of school-wide values rather than individual ones.

The school creates a sense of community whose values are shared by all. This does not imply a conflict with the individual or child-centred pedagogical approach of recent times. It means rather that each member of the school is conscious of its special identity and common purpose.

ix) Maximum use of learning time.

Students must be enabled to spend the maximum amount of time in active learning. There should be a minimum of interruption between and within classes. Articulation between subject areas and sequences of learning should be used to avoid duplication and unnecessary repetition.

x) The active and substantial support of the responsible education authority.

The school is confident of the support of its education authority not only in terms of the necessary financial contribution but also of leadership and guidance.

Six comments need to be made about the above list. First, it is deliberately pared down to stark essentials; each characteristic could become the subject of a disquisition. The literature on effective schools is already voluminous and no point would be served here in trying even to summarise it. Second, all the characteristics have been referred to at some point in preceding chapters. Third, some characteristics are more influential than others. Thus, the first one concerning the commitment to clearly-defined goals might be considered a precondition for all the rest. Fourth, some of the characteristics can be interpreted more or less broadly. This is notably true of the notion of leadership. Fifth, most of the characteristics could equally apply to any social organisation and, indeed, some of those writing about effective schools acknowledge their debt to organisational theory. Sixth, the research has relied heavily, though not exclusively, on North American findings. This automatically limits the degree of variation in the wider environments in which the schools studied operate as well as the organisational arrangements of which they are part. These characteristics are not necessarily universal, therefore, and at the least, the weighting of each will vary from one system to another.

Baldly stated, the characteristics might appear so self-evident as to raise the question why it has been necessary to undertake so much research in order to identify them. The reality is, however, that few schools possess all ten characteristics and some schools do not possess a single one of them. The latter proposition can be verified by expressing each characteristic negatively and seeing how many schools then emerge with a totally adverse record. In other words, the apparently obvious goes largely unheeded. Research findings come to the aid of common-sense perceptions in identifying what are the characteristics of an effective school. The subjective evidence, which has so often been dismissed as prejudiced or merely impressionistic, is reinforced. No school has the excuse of not knowing what it should be like.

These ten characteristics are not separated from one another in practice but overlap and interact. Nor can they be taken for granted. A school that relaxes over even one characteristic is likely to deteriorate, and deterioration can set in with dismaying rapidity. No school can therefore afford to accept a static state but must rather ceaselessly assure that its goals are being achieved and take swift action whenever it identifies an incipient weakness.

Functions of education authorities

If it is a hard and unremitting task for a good school to maintain favourable conditions, it is still more difficult for a bad school to transform itself into a good one. For one thing, the spur to transformation must come from the outside. Here the role of the responsible education authority is critical. It alone is in a position to monitor all the schools within its jurisdiction and to react when any school is found to be performing unsatisfactorily. Besides continuing to offer leadership and guidance instructively in a spirit of partnership it must then intervene decisively to facilitate change.

The notion of *facilitating* rather than enforcing change needs to be emphasised for, it must be reiterated, no school can be radically changed by means of external action. Most of the characteristics of the good school grow out of and depend for their continuity on internal dynamics. External intervention has limited power to influence those dynamics and a long time may ensue before results are seen even in those areas where it is influential.

Among the critical functions that education authorities can exercise are to:

    i)   arouse and sustain a pervasive public concern about the quality of education;
   ii)   specify clearly what society expects all its schools to achieve;
  iii)   lay down a core curriculum for all students and the terms under which optional subjects should be offered;

- *iv)* ensure that teachers undergo an effective initial training and have ample opportunities for continuing professional development;
- *v)* prescribe sound management structures for schools that include the participation of parents and community representatives;
- *vi)* ensure that all schools have adequate resources;
- *vii)* monitor the performance of schools with a view to ensuring that overall standards are satisfactory and that ineffective schools are identified and compelled to improve;
- *viii)* protect the freedom of each and every school.

It is obvious that how these are interpreted and realised in practice will vary considerably depending on the organisational arrangements and distribution of decision-making power in each national system.

Part three

SUMMARY AND CONCLUSIONS

QUALITY: THE NEW PRIORITY

Concern for the quality of education in schools is today among the highest priorities in all OECD countries; it will no doubt remain so for the foreseeable future.

But there are no instant remedies for raising quality nor is it a one-off exercise. In many education systems, it is rather a question of consolidating the numerous reforms of recent years and making painstaking efforts over a long haul to bring about improvements in every aspect of schooling. In some systems, however, it may call for radical departures from established arrangements and practices.

An outstanding difficulty is that the concept of quality is so widely interpreted, both within and across countries, as to defy exact analysis. Given that, it would be futile for the OECD to propose a tight and universally-accepted definition but it is important to attempt to clarify the concept itself and to understand the implications of adopting different interpretations of it. The concept of quality is a complex one.

A useful route into this complexity is to analyse the reasons for this new-found concern; such analysis reveals a complex variety of public concerns and new pressures resulting in criticisms at unprecedented levels. The report points out, however, that criticisms are always more readily identifiable and newsworthy than general public satisfaction with schooling.

REASONS FOR CONCERN ABOUT SCHOOL QUALITY

Reactions to an era of growth

Societies reacted against the optimism of the sixties and early seventies when education systems underwent rapid expansion and educational development was seen as a key determinant of the generation of wealth and the realisation of social equality. That reaction intensified with the advent of high rates of youth unemployment, heightening the realisation that many young people are leaving school poorly prepared for adult and working life. In some countries, there was alleged evidence of a decline in educational attainment levels. At the same time, participation in educational decision-making broadened with different interest groups developing articulate claims about aims and policies for schools.

After an initial negative, even pessimistic, reaction, there are now signs of greater optimism and a renewal of belief in education's key contribution to economic and social well-being. Public expectations of schools are high. For all these reasons and reactions, positive and negative, education is exposed to searching public scrutiny. It is expected to be fully accountable to society for what it does and to give value for money. This means an intense focus on the quality of what schools provide.

Sharper public scrutiny of education would in all probability have taken place, sooner or later, irrespective of the economic reversal of the seventies that so abruptly diminished the optimism of the previous decade. The two dominant features of the earlier period — expansion (quantitative growth) and the widening of educational access to new clienteles (equality of opportunity) — would have brought with them the demand for taking stock and the reassertion of qualitative alongside quantitative considerations.

Reforms of process not just of educational structures

Structural reforms of systems have been shown to have limited power to resolve perennial educational issues, notably to ensure equality of opportunity for all. The overriding difficulty is how, within different structural arrangements, to transform pedagogical practices and to bring about the active involvement in innovation of all the actors in the teaching/learning process. This creates the necessity of having a deeper understanding of what actually takes place within schools — the quality of the teaching and learning that takes place there.

An outstanding problem concerns the inability of reforms to affect the sizeable minority of students who gain little from their schooling. How are schools to uphold the principle that all young people should be introduced to a common culture and guaranteed equal access to the upper reaches of the education system? How is the rising pressure to keep all young people ever longer in school to be satisfied without jeopardising the academic ambitions of the more scholastic or failing to provide appropriate learning opportunities either for the wide range of students of average abilities or for those who presently get least out of their schooling?

Economic and social demands

Acknowledgement of the importance of "human capital" in economic development has re-emerged and with it renewed emphasis on the value of education and training. However, particular attention is now being paid to the qualitative demand for labour raising strongly the argument that this requires a workforce that has correspondingly high-quality knowledge and skills. Similarly, the necessity of being internationally competitive has caused the spotlight to fall on relative educational performance.

The implications for schooling, however, need to be clarified. There remain sizeable lacuna in understanding its precise contribution to economic well-being, which will necessarily be long-term and will often operate indirectly rather than in visible and direct ways. This fact alone exposes schools to criticisms when the political pressure is frequently for immediate results. At the same time, it is to be stressed that the duty of schools to provide a sound preparation for adult life does not detract from the essential role of recurrent education and training in responding immediately to rapid structural and occupational change. Schools should not be blamed for all observed deficiencies of knowledge and skills, nor do all solutions necessarily lie within their ambit.

Schools today are beset by a plethora of new functions and conflicting pressures. They must demonstrate that they are adequately discharging the tasks of teaching, socialisation, and child care that they have acquired while adapting to the changing external environment

— the impact of the media, the knowledge explosion, family break-downs — that is encroaching on their traditionally enclosed status. More is expected of them even as their freedom of action is increasingly constrained by the pressures for external accountability.

In responding to rising social expectations, education systems must strike a balance between demonstrating a genuine concern for public accountability and maintaining the creative autonomy of schools and the responsible professionalism of teachers.

DIFFERENT APPROACHES TO QUALITY

Apart from the different meanings of the word "quality" itself, that include both the descriptive and the normative, there are different dimensions of the concept when specifically applied to education and a variety of approaches have been adopted to define and improve quality in schooling. Such differences are inevitable given that the focus of educational debate and practical action varies from the most local "micro" level of the school and classroom through to that of the education system as a whole. These are also only a corollary of the subjective nature of the concept and the politically-charged debate about how quality can best be raised.

The report attempts to clarify these many aspects of the quality issue by addressing four broad and overlapping questions:

— What level of schooling — macro or micro — is under scrutiny and what is the inspiration of that scrutiny — committed political reform or detached academic analysis?
— What are appropriate goals and objectives, how broadly should they extend beyond those specifically to do with student learning, and how are priorities among them to be determined when matters are in dispute?
— Quality of what — how far does the concern for improvement embrace non-cognitive goals?
— Quality and equality — quality for whom?

Aims and priorities

Definitions of quality are crucially determined by educational aims. Yet, since those aims are general statements of desired outcomes, then, as with health or economic well-being, there is always room for improvement. Quality can always be better. Aims do not, therefore, provide absolute criteria to judge when quality is satisfactory.

Two potentially conflicting ideas tend to be confounded in the current interest in quality: on the one hand, that there should be a shift of priority from inputs (including financial resources) to outputs; on the other, that the complex chemistry of schooling defies the application of simplistic input-output models. It would be mistaken to argue that a revived focus on outcomes implies that the inputs and processes that determine them become accordingly less important; both are crucial.

Advocates of closer attention to outcomes must clarify whether priority is to be given to those that are specifically cognitive or whether desired ends should equally cover the broader purposes of education to include affective, social, aesthetic, and moral learning. Since all systems agree that the range of aims for schools is broad, this is a matter of deciding priorities.

Priorities must be set, too, concerning the target groups of policies. For some, the quality issue is about nothing if it is not about the low-achiever; for others, it is predominantly about the gifted and high-achievers; others again insist that it concerns *all* pupils in *all* schools. Priorities for the gifted or the low-achievers should not be set at the expense of the large middle group of pupils whose talents are clustered around the average.

The changing terms of educational debate

The search for clarity is rendered increasingly problematic by the fact that so many educational ideas and innovations have been tried over the last two decades, evaluated, and shown to be less than ideal. There exists today an "informed scepticism" about educational change that distinguishes the 1980s from the 1960s and has led to the declining appeal of grand principles and all-embracing educational theories. A major benefit of amassing research and observation is that simplistic recipes for improvement can be exposed as flawed, but the opposite danger is that bold solutions go unrecognised. The traditional contrasting ideologies of educational debate — conservative versus progressive, elitist versus egalitarian, right versus left — are increasingly inadequate terms to apply to today's complex debate and the concern for improving quality spans these different divides.

Quality and equality

Considerations of how quality and equality should be interpreted and realised interact very closely. In some regards, there may be a tension between their broad aims, in other ways, they are directly complementary. The call for closer attention to cognitive outcomes should not be regarded as inimical to improving the opportunities and performance of low-achievers; indeed, it is a precondition of that improvement.

The question "quality for whom?" goes beyond the application of universal standards and the resulting identification of low achievement, and asks how well school systems are at present responding to the educational claims of different social and cultural groups as they themselves formulate those claims. Giving priority to that question, therefore, provides a far-reaching interpretation of equality of opportunity based on the degree of participation in the running of schools and school policy. To avoid a political free-for-all, the special claims should, where possible, be integrated into the normal practice of schooling.

The standards question

There are a number of meanings of the term "standards". Commonly they are equated with average attainment levels. They may also be interpreted as societal expectations and as educational aims. The more precise the contents given to standards, the more do they provide guidelines for assessment while possibly also being open to the charge of partiality.

How evidence is used to illuminate the debate on standards depends crucially not only on the interpretation that is adopted but also on educational ideologies and values. The use of scientific evidence is thus too often predetermined yet recognition of that fact cannot leave the way open to purely ideological debate. Empirical evidence should be deployed as extensively as possible to establish matters of fact.

Equating standards with average attainment levels should avoid confounding what *should be* with what *is*, and any conclusions based on such averages ought to recognise fully how sensitive are findings to the measures and measuring instruments used. Care must be taken to avoid assuming that evidence on single indicators stand as adequate proxies for performance in all relevant areas of knowledge, skills, and competence.

Assessment of whether standards are rising or falling is far from straightforward. Among the complexities are the formidable technical and educational problems of assessing change and of fixing bench-marks against which progress or decline takes place. Even if those trends seem relatively well established, it still leaves to be answered both what are the most important underlying *causes* and what policy measures will have the most pronounced *impact* on further improvement.

Evidence about the views and attitudes of the schools' different users is an important complement to measures of achievement so that aims can be clarified and satisfaction levels assessed. Subjective attitudes are, nevertheless, shaped by objective factors and the evidence about them suggests not only that external expectations of schools are rising but that they are diverse and sometimes contradictory. The views of students themselves are especially important.

Enquiry into *trends* in standards is thus fraught with technical, conceptual, and political problems. Of greater priority is:

  i) the engagement in a society-wide process of clarifying *contemporary* standards and establishing how satisfactory is current performance in terms of those standards;
  ii) the development of statistics and indicators specifically designed to assist that process;
  iii) enquiry, research, and debate concerning the *effects* on those standards of particular educational arrangements and mooted reforms.

KEY AREAS IN THE PURSUIT OF QUALITY IN SCHOOLS AND SYSTEMS

The curriculum

How the curriculum is defined, planned, implemented, and evaluated, crucially influences the quality of the education that is provided.

The most important curriculum issue concerns the idea of a *core* for a key condition of quality in education is that all children, regardless of sex, ethnic origin, or where they happen to live, should be taught essential knowledge and skills up to an acceptable level of achievement. The exact composition of the core will be different from country to country or region to region within countries and will differ over time as priorities are reordered.

There is no necessary contradiction between the idea of a common core curriculum and giving individual students the opportunity of choosing from a variety of modules. Such a curriculum design can be effectively based on the principle that there may be several equally valid routes into the common curriculum. One of the important functions of schools is to provide students with adequate guidance when making their choices: schools and teachers have a duty to negotiate a balanced curriculum; choice does not have to be unrestrained.

Preparation for working life, broadly conceived, must inform the core curriculum, especially at the secondary level. General education should include such matters as teaching and guidance about working life and training requirements, the mechanics of the labour market, and the role of enterprises in the national economy.

The use of objectives in curriculum planning, at different levels — national, regional, school, classroom — can be a constructive way of improving schooling simply by focusing more sharply on certain areas of learning and linking evaluation with teaching.

Assessment, evaluation, and monitoring

It is essential not only to identify what a student does not understand, but also to attempt to discover the source of the lack of understanding so that it can be remedied. In this the diagnostic role of the teacher is crucial.

One of the dangers that national and school curriculum planning should counteract is the tendency for educational institutions to become dominated by their assessment techniques. Given that caveat, graded tests have a place in a rationally-planned curriculum evaluation scheme. Criterion-referenced tests or examinations have certain advantages: for one thing, they specify standards or criteria that every student should attain. Profiling is valuable when used as a means of assessing performance across the whole curriculum.

School-based evaluation, a process by which teachers discuss the functioning of their own school as a group of professionals in such a way as to bring about improvement, is a critical element in the pursuit of quality.

One way of monitoring education systems is through a corps of inspectors, whose role and functions still need clarification in many countries.

Relying on parental choice is being advocated in some quarters as a way of evaluating schools that depends on the views of clients rather than professionals. But it can run counter to some of the contemporary goals of education. The reality remains that in democratic societies parents will always exercise some degree of educational choice for their children. The aim should be to ensure that society's overall goals and the wishes of individual parents coincide as much as possible.

In education systems, the process of evaluation and accountability is two-way: the central authority must have adequate channels of communication to inform schools about policy decisions, but the policy-makers must also be sensitive to the views of teachers and parents. Similarly, policy-makers need to have reliable and regular information about standards in schools, and to be constantly assured about the level of quality.

Many countries concur that part of the process of improving quality in education is to make available national and international data on various aspects of educational standards. This depends on agreeing what standards are, being able to measure them, and ensuring that the means do not distort the ends.

The role of teachers

The competence and commitment of teachers are the vital prerequisites for producing an education of quality. Yet in many OECD countries at the present time, there is public discontent with the performance of teachers while many teachers are manifestly unhappy with their lot.

Teachers find themselves in the firing line of new challenges and pressures. Some are suffering from a crisis of professional identity. Many are overstretched. It is less and less clear what the good teacher is supposed to be.

A four-pronged approach is called for:

   i) Attract good recruits;
   ii) Prepare new teachers more effectively;
   iii) Take measures to maintain the competence of practising teachers;
   iv) Generally seek to raise teacher morale and motivation.

The aim must be to recruit teachers of the highest possible calibre. This means having not only a very clear conception of what constitutes the good teacher but one that is compatible with the variety of teaching methods, pedagogical approaches, personality and style. In selecting teachers, particular attention must be paid to personality factors as well as to academic qualifications, for the way a teacher relates to students and interacts with them is crucial for successful teaching and learning.

Salaries must be sufficiently attractive to permit competition with other professions and business enterprises. It is impossible, however, in many countries to offer salary scales comparable with many of those on offer. A high premium is placed, therefore, on job satisfaction, good conditions of service, and a recognised status in society. If progress is not forthcoming on either front, it will not be surprising if countries fail to attract sufficient numbers of high-quality entrants to teaching.

Part of the initial training problem is that there is simply too much information to acquire and too many skills to learn in the limited time available; initial training, therefore, has to be seen as the first stage of professional preparation, not the whole of it.

In-service education should be provided on a more uniform basis and made available to all teachers, including those in remote areas. It should be provided systematically, with a meaningful sequence built into the provision rather than a set of haphazard choices, however rich they may be. It should offer a clear advantage to each teacher concerned, as well as to his or her school and to the educational service as a whole.

If salaries remain relatively low and promotion prospects limited, other ways should be found of providing professional satisfaction by means of a combination of staff development and an attractive career structure.

Teachers as well as parents and policy-makers would benefit from tighter definitions of professional competence. It is important, therefore, that teachers should be regarded as professionals, submitting their expertise to regular appraisal, and in extreme cases of incompetence being transferred to other duties. The primary purpose of appraisal should be to foster professional development and it will probably be effective only if teachers themselves are closely involved in the appraisal process.

School organisation

However the experience of schooling may be divided into cycles, there is a need for continuity from one year or module and one cycle to the next. The curriculum should be so designed as to build links or bridges between each stage. Class teachers might accompany the same students through two or more years of schooling. There might be regular contacts and co-ordinated curriculum planning between those teaching at the different levels. Detailed records of students might be kept charting their progress and giving each new teacher an accurate picture of their strengths and weaknesses.

School size is a significant factor in determining the teaching and learning environment.

Small schools create a friendly atmosphere and a sense of community whereas large schools can offer a wider choice of subjects and opportunities for extra-curricular activities. It is important to attempt to combine both by various forms of internal organisation and the sharing of facilities, wherever possible, among smaller schools.

Excessive class size is a barrier to effective teaching and, wherever possible, classes should be small enough to permit the teacher to give attention to each student. However, in some circumstances, it may be more beneficial to devote additional resources to other purposes than reducing class size.

It is important to ensure that the number of hours each teacher spends with a class in a week and the number of students with whom each teacher comes into contact during a single day or week, help to facilitate rather than hinder the learning process.

The amount of time students spend in school is only significant for learning outcomes if that time is utilised to the best possible advantage.

The popular impression of the value of homework does appear to be reinforced by empirical evidence. However, ways and means must be found of helping deprived children to study outside regular school hours if they are not to fall further behind.

Individual countries and autonomous local authorities may find it salutary to compare their aggregrate attendance requirements for students with those prevailing elsewhere.

Psychological research and common-sense experience combine to suggest that different ways of organising the school day, term, and year be considered; this may well include looking at the benefits of shorter terms and more frequent and shorter breaks.

The resources dimension

It is difficult to come by compelling empirical evidence that shows a strong direct correlation between resource inputs and school outputs even as measured by standardized achievements in tests. This is because the way resources are used and the environments of schools can vary so greatly that quantitative analyses are unlikely to show consistent effects. It does not mean that resources "don't matter". Some education authorities, national, regional and local, consider that improving quality does require greater resources. Thus, several countries have opted to invest savings from falling school enrolments in qualitative improvements.

At the present time, most school systems cannot hope to obtain significantly greater resources, while they are under pressure to demonstrate that they are exacting full value from those that are already available. Paradoxically, most of the specific recommendations for improving the quality of schooling, including those proposed by value-for-money advocates, postulate increased expenditure, sometimes on a large scale.

Four proposals are in vogue for improving standards without necessarily increasing costs: to deploy staff and resources more effectively; to attract or increase parental and other external contributions; to make economies by using new instructional technologies; to rely, at least partially, on consumer preferences. None of these proposals is without problems, but each is worth serious consideration.

It is necessary for all the actors in education to become cost-conscious, to strive to make economies wherever possible, and to ensure that resources are used where they will result in the maximum possible learning gains.

The physical, and not only financial, resources of buildings and facilities are indispensable and too often taken for granted. It is especially important that they are not neglected in the face of cutbacks in capital expenditures; just as the effects of such neglect may not be immediately apparent, so will they be difficult to remedy once problems emerge.

THE SCHOOL AS THE HEART OF THE MATTER

A substantial body of recent research has taken the form of in-depth observations in classrooms and schools and produced two important related findings: *a)* that student motivation and achievement are profoundly affected by the distinctive culture or ethos that is to be found in each school; *b)* that schools in which students perform well have all or nearly all a number of identifiable characteristics.

Ten characteristics appear to play a particularly powerful role in determining desirable school outcomes:

- *i)* a commitment to clearly and commonly identified norms and goals;
- *ii)* collaborative planning, shared decision-making, and collegial work in a frame of experimentation and evaluation;
- *iii)* positive leadership in initiating and maintaining improvement;
- *iv)* staff stability;
- *v)* a strategy for continuing staff development related to each school's pedagogical and organisational needs;
- *vi)* working to a carefully planned and co-ordinated curriculum that ensures sufficient place for each student to acquire essential knowledge and skills;
- *vii)* a high level of parental involvement and support;
- *viii)* the pursuit and recognition of school-wide values rather than individual ones;
- *ix)* maximum use of learning time;
- *x)* the active and substantial support of the responsible education authority.

Few would restrict the definition of school quality purely to the academic criteria on which "effectiveness" in the literature commonly depends; the lessons of that literature nevertheless provide valuable pointers to the general pursuit of school improvement.

Among the critical functions that education authorities can exercise, the most important include:

- *i)* to arouse and sustain a pervasive public concern about the quality of education;
- *ii)* to specify clearly what society expects all its schools to achieve;
- *iii)* to lay down a core curriculum for all students and the terms under which optional subjects should be offered;
- *iv)* to ensure that teachers undergo an effective initial training and have ample opportunities for continuing professional development;
- *v)* to prescribe sound management structures for schools that include the participation of parents and community representatives;
- *vi)* to ensure that all schools have adequate resources;
- *vii)* to monitor the performance of schools with a view to ensuring that overall standards are satisfactory and that ineffective schools are identified and compelled to improve;
- *viii)* to protect the freedom of each and every school.

WHERE TO OBTAIN OECD PUBLICATIONS
OÙ OBTENIR LES PUBLICATIONS DE L'OCDE

ARGENTINA – ARGENTINE
Carlos Hirsch S.R.L.,
Galería Guemes, Florida 165, 4° Piso,
1333 Buenos Aires   Tel. 30.7122, 331.1787 y 331.2391
Telegram.: Hirsch-Baires

AUSTRALIA – AUSTRALIE
D.A. Book (Aust.) Pty. Ltd.
11-13 Station Street (P.O. Box 163)
Mitcham, Vic. 3132   Tel. (03) 873 4411
Telex: AA37911 DA BOOK   Telefax: (03)873.5679

AUSTRIA – AUTRICHE
OECD Publications and Information Centre,
4 Simrockstrasse,
5300 Bonn (Germany)   Tel. (0228) 21.60.45
Telex: 8 86300 Bonn   Telefax: (0228)26.11.04
Gerold & Co., Graben 31, Wien 1   Tel. (1)533.50.14

BELGIUM – BELGIQUE
Jean de Lannoy, Avenue du Roi 202
B-1060 Bruxelles   Tel. (02) 538.51.69/538.08.41
Telex: 63220

CANADA
Renouf Publishing Company Ltd
1294 Algoma Road, Ottawa, Ont. K1B 3W8
   Tel: (613) 741-4333
Telex: 053-4783   Telefax: (613)741.5439
Stores:
61 Sparks St., Ottawa, Ont. K1P 5R1
   Tel: (613) 238-8985
211 rue Yonge St., Toronto, Ont. M5B 1M4
   Tel: (416) 363-3171
Federal Publications Inc.,
165 University Avenue,
Toronto, ON M5H 3B9   Tel. (416)581-1552
Telefax: (416)581.1743
Les Publications Fédérales
1185 rue de l'Université
Montréal, PQ H3B 1R7   Tel.(514)954.1633
Les Éditions la Liberté Inc.,
3020 Chemin Sainte-Foy,
Sainte-Foy, P.Q. G1X 3V6,   Tel. (418)658-3763
Telefax: (418)658.3763

DENMARK – DANEMARK
Munksgaard Export and Subscription Service
35, Nørre Søgade, P.O. Box 212148
DK-1016 København K   Tel. (45 1)12.85.70
Telex: 19431 MUNKS DK   Telefax: (45 1)12.93.87

FINLAND – FINLANDE
Akateeminen Kirjakauppa,
Keskuskatu 1, P.O. Box 128
00100 Helsinki   Tel. (358 0)12141
Telex: 125080   Telefax: (358 0)121.4441

FRANCE
OCDE/OECD
Mail Orders/Commandes par correspondance :
2, rue André-Pascal,
75775 Paris Cedex 16   Tel. (1) 45.24.82.00
Bookshop/Librairie : 33, rue Octave-Feuillet
75016 Paris
   Tel. (1) 45.24.81.67 or/ou (1) 45.24.81.81
Telex: 620 160 OCDE   Telefax: (33-1)45.24.85.00
Librairie de l'Université,
12a, rue Nazareth,
13602 Aix-en-Provence   Tel. 42.26.18.08

GERMANY – ALLEMAGNE
OECD Publications and Information Centre,
4 Simrockstrasse,
5300 Bonn   Tel. (0228) 21.60.45
Telex: 8 86300 Bonn   Telefax: (0228)26.11.04

GREECE – GRÈCE
Librairie Kauffmann,
28, rue du Stade, 105 64 Athens   Tel. 322.21.60
Telex: 218187 LIKA Gr

HONG KONG
Government Information Services,
Publications (Sales) Office,
Information Services Department
No. 1, Battery Path, Central
Tel.(5)23.31.91   Telex: 802.61190

ICELAND – ISLANDE
Mál Mog Menning
Laugavegi 18, Pósthólf 392
121 Reykjavik   Tel. 15199/24240

INDIA – INDE
Oxford Book and Stationery Co.,
Scindia House,
New Delhi 110001   Tel. 331.5896/5308
Telex: 31 61990 AM IN   Telefax: (11) 332.5993
17 Park St., Calcutta 700016   Tel. 240832

INDONESIA – INDONÉSIE
Pdii-Lipi, P.O. Box 3065/JKT.
Jakarta   Tel. 583467
Telex: 73 45875

IRELAND – IRLANDE
TDC Publishers - Library Suppliers,
12 North Frederick Street,
Dublin 1   Tel. 744835-749677
Telex: 33530TDCP EI Telefax: 748416

ITALY – ITALIE
Libreria Commissionaria Sansoni,
Via Benedetto Fortini 120/10,
Casella Post. 552
50125 Firenze   Tel. (055)645415
Telex: 570466   Telefax: (39.55)641257
Via Bartolini 29, 20155 Milano   Tel. 365083
La diffusione delle pubblicazioni OCSE viene assicurata
dalle principali librerie ed anche da :
Editrice e Libreria Herder,
Piazza Montecitorio 120, 00186 Roma
Tel. 6794628   Telex: NATEL I 621427
Libreria Hœpli,
Via Hœpli 5, 20121 Milano   Tel. 865446
Telex:31.33.95   Telefax: (39.2)805.2886
Libreria Scientifica
Dott. Lucio de Biasio "Aeiou"
Via Meravigli 16, 20123 Milano   Tel. 807679
Telefax: 800175

JAPAN – JAPON
OECD Publications and Information Centre,
Landic Akasaka Building, 2-3-4 Akasaka,
Minato-ku, Tokyo 107   Tel. 586.2016
   Telefax: (81.3) 584.7929

KOREA – CORÉE
Kyobo Book Centre Co. Ltd.
P.O.Box 1658, Kwang Hwa Moon
Seoul   Tel. (REP) 730.78.91
Telefax: 735.0030

MALAYSIA/SINGAPORE – MALAISIE/SINGAPOUR
University of Malaya Co-operative Bookshop Ltd.,
P.O. Box 1127, Jalan Pantai Baru 59100
Kuala Lumpur, Malaysia/Malaisie
Tel. 756.5000/756.5425   Telefax: 757.3661
Information Publications Pte Ltd
Pei-Fu Industrial Building,
24 New Industrial Road No. 02-06
Singapore/Singapour 1953   Tel. 283.1786/283.1798
Telefax: 284.8875

NETHERLANDS – PAYS-BAS
SDU Uitgeverij
Christoffel Plantijnstraat 2
Postbus 20014
2500 EA's-Gravenhage   Tel. (070)78.99.11
Voor bestellingen: Tel. (070)78.98.80
Telex: 32486 stdru   Telefax: (070)47.63.51

NEW ZEALAND – NOUVELLE-ZÉLANDE
Government Printing Office Bookshops:
Auckland: Retail Bookshop, 25 Rutland Street,
Mail Orders, 85 Beach Road
Private Bag C.P.O.
Hamilton: Retail: Ward Street,
Mail Orders, P.O. Box 857
Wellington: Retail, Mulgrave Street, (Head Office)
Cubacade World Trade Centre,
Mail Orders, Private Bag
Christchurch: Retail, 159 Hereford Street,
Mail Orders, Private Bag
Dunedin: Retail, Princes Street,
Mail Orders, P.O. Box 1104

NORWAY – NORVÈGE
Narvesen Info Center – NIC,
Bertrand Narvesens vei 2,
P.O.B. 6125 Etterstad, 0602 Oslo 6
   Tel. (02)67.83.10/(02)68.40.20
Telex: 79668 NIC N   Telefax: (47 2)68.53.47

PAKISTAN
Mirza Book Agency
65 Shahrah Quaid-E-Azam, Lahore 3   Tel. 66839
Telegram: "Knowledge"

PORTUGAL
Livraria Portugal, Rua do Carmo 70-74,
1117 Lisboa Codex   Tel. 347.49.82/3/4/5

SINGAPORE/MALAYSIA – SINGAPOUR/MALAISIE
See "Malaysia/Singapore". Voir « Malaisie/Singapour »

SPAIN – ESPAGNE
Mundi-Prensa Libros, S.A.,
Castelló 37, Apartado 1223,
Madrid-28001   Tel. 431.33.99
Telex: 49370 MPLI   Telefax: 275.39.98
Libreria Bosch, Ronda Universidad 11,
Barcelona 7   Tel. 317.53.08/317.53.58

SWEDEN – SUÈDE
Fritzes Fackboksföretaget
Box 16356, S 103 27 STH,
Regeringsgatan 12,
DS Stockholm   Tel. (08)23.89.00
Telex: 12387   Telefax: (08)20.50.21
Subscription Agency/Abonnements:
Wennergren-Williams AB,
Box 30004, S104 25 Stockholm   Tel. (08)54.12.00
Telex: 19937   Telefax: (08)50.82.86

SWITZERLAND – SUISSE
OECD Publications and Information Centre,
4 Simrockstrasse,
5300 Bonn (Germany)   Tel. (0228) 21.60.45
Telex: 8 86300 Bonn   Telefax: (0228)26.11.04
Librairie Payot,
6 rue Grenus, 1211 Genève 11   Tel. (022)731.89.50
Telex: 28356
Maditec S.A.
Ch. des Palettes 4
1020 – Renens/Lausanne   Tel. (021)635.08.65
Telefax: (021)635.07.80
United Nations Bookshop/Librairie des Nations-Unies
Palais des Nations, 1211 – Geneva 10
   Tel. (022)734.60.11 (ext. 48.72)
Telex: 289696 (Attn: Sales)   Telefax: (022)733.98.79

TAIWAN – FORMOSE
Good Faith Worldwide Int'l Co., Ltd.
9th floor, No. 118, Sec.2, Chung Hsiao E. Road
Taipei   Tel. 391.7396/391.7397
Telefax: 394.9176

THAILAND – THAÏLANDE
Suksit Siam Co., Ltd., 1715 Rama IV Rd.,
Samyam, Bangkok 5   Tel. 2511630

TURKEY – TURQUIE
Kültur Yayinlari Is-Türk Ltd. Sti.
Atatürk Bulvari No. 191/Kat. 21
Kavaklidere/Ankara   Tel. 25.07.60
Dolmabahce Cad. No. 29
Besiktas/Istanbul   Tel. 160.71.88
Telex: 43482B

UNITED KINGDOM – ROYAUME-UNI
H.M. Stationery Office   (01)873-8483
Postal orders only:
P.O.B. 276, London SW8 5DT
Telephone orders: (01) 873-9090, or
Personal callers:
49 High Holborn, London WC1V 6HB
Telex:297138   Telefax: 873.8463
Branches at: Belfast, Birmingham, Bristol, Edinburgh,
Manchester

UNITED STATES – ÉTATS-UNIS
OECD Publications and Information Centre,
2001 L Street, N.W., Suite 700,
Washington, D.C. 20036-4095   Tel. (202)785.6323
Telex:440245 WASHINGTON D.C.
Telefax: (202)785.0350

VENEZUELA
Libreria del Este,
Avda F. Miranda 52, Aptdo. 60337,
Edificio Galipan, Caracas 106
   Tel. 951.1705/951.2307/951.1297
Telegram: Libreste Caracas

YUGOSLAVIA – YOUGOSLAVIE
Jugoslovenska Knjiga, Knez Mihajlova 2,
P.O.B. 36, Beograd   Tel. 621.992
Telex: 12466 jk bgd

Orders and inquiries from countries where Distributors
have not yet been appointed should be sent to: OECD,
Publications Service, 2, rue André-Pascal, 75775 PARIS
CEDEX 16.

Les commandes provenant de pays où l'OCDE n'a pas
encore désigné de distributeur devraient être adressées à :
OCDE, Service des Publications, 2, rue André-Pascal,
75775 PARIS CEDEX 16.

72547-6-1989

OECD PUBLICATIONS, 2, rue André-Pascal, 75775 PARIS CEDEX 16 - No. 44661 1989
PRINTED IN FRANCE
(91 89 02 1) ISBN 92-64-13254-6